I0161271

FORWARD

By
Evelyn Wagner

TEACH Services, Inc.

P U B L I S H I N G

www.TEACHServices.com

World rights reserved. This book or any portion thereof may not be copied or reproduced in any form or manner whatever, except as provided by law, without the written permission of the publisher, except by a reviewer who may quote brief passages in a review.

This book was written to provide truthful information in regard to the subject matter covered. The author assumes full responsibility for the accuracy of all facts and quotations as cited in this book. The opinions expressed in this book are the author's personal views and interpretation of the Bible, Spirit of Prophecy, and/or contemporary authors and do not necessarily reflect those of TEACH Services, Inc.

This book is sold with the understanding that the publisher is not engaged in giving spiritual, legal, medical, or other professional advice. If authoritative advice is needed, the reader should seek the counsel of a competent professional.

Copyright © 2009, Revised 2012 TEACH Services, Inc.
ISBN-13: 978-1-57258-602-4 (Paperback)
ISBN-13: 978-1-57258-835-6 (ePub)
ISBN-13: 978-1-57258-836-3 (Kindle/Mobi)

Library of Congress Control Number: 2009937802

Published by
TEACH Services, Inc.
P U B L I S H I N G
www.TEACHServices.com

Dedication

This book is dedicated to
The best Friend a person can have, Jesus.
He parts the Red Sea of trials
So His people can walk through
With confidence and peace.
He opens doors of opportunity
And breaks down the walls set up by Satan
To stop all progress.
God opens the windows of heaven
With a mighty hand
So His work can go "Forward."
Praise His Name.

CHAPTER 1

It was a stormy Tuesday afternoon, December 8, 1987, when the loaded aircraft lifted into the clear blue sky. It rose above the dark clouds that were dumping buckets of water onto the small Medford, Oregon, airfield below. The waiting had been long and tiring, sitting in the crowded departure lounge in the airport hour after hour. A storm was covering the Northwest. Now one landing strip was open at the San Francisco Airport. Delmer and Evelyn were heading straight for that airstrip.

Several months before, Delmer had convinced Evelyn that if they would get a satellite dish there would be hundreds of programs to choose from with many good programs worth watching. After purchasing the dish, he was disappointed in the programs—until he discovered Three Angels Broadcasting Network (3ABN), a new Christian network.

"Lift up the trumpet and loud let it ring. Jesus is coming again." The words from the familiar hymn reminded them that now their time was not their own. Overnight the television screen took control of their lives as they watched it, recorded it, and gave the recordings to friends and relatives.

"Everyone should be getting these programs." Delmer repeated over and over. "We need to get a station here and pick up 3ABN to send to everyone in this valley. No, what really should be done is to get the church leadership involved and have stations all over North America. We could do it. It isn't that hard. I need to contact the church leaders of every conference in North America and let them know of the possibility of every community having their own television station."

Delmer borrowed the *Seventh-day Adventist Yearbook* from Pastor Charles Betz and started dictating letters.

"The Federal Communications Commission (FCC) has changed the ruling. It is now possible for churches to have a television station in almost any community. Other church denominations are getting their own stations. Why aren't we? Something must be done." Delmer stated his concerns to everyone who would listen and to a few who would rather not.

Every Seventh-day Adventist conference in North America received a letter stressing the fact that this may well be the time God would have our message go to all of the communities in the United States, with programs from our schools, hospitals, and Three Angels Broadcasting Network.

The few letters that staggered back were good at pointing out every negative thing available—real and imaginary! Some friends were mildly supportive. Some thought it was an impossible dream. And others? Well—Evelyn asked Delmer to please not talk about the TV so much, or maybe soon they would not have any friends left! He was so excited about the subject she felt he was beginning to sound like a recording machine stuck on one spot. However, asking him not to talk about Christian TV was like asking the birds not to sing!

In spite of little encouragement, Delmer went forward and had a study made to see which channels were available in the Rogue River Valley. He applied for a construction permit with the FCC for a channel in Grants Pass and for another one in Rogue River. He lost the one in Grants Pass to someone else—a chance one always has to take. Next, he changed Channel 65 from Rogue River to Grants Pass and applied for another one for Rogue River. As each day passed, he became more wound up about the possibilities available.

Applying for a television permit is costly and time consuming. Applications must be filled out completely and correctly with information that takes hours to obtain. One little mistake throws the whole application out. It seemed like a slow learning process to Evelyn as she typed one application form after another. There were deadlines to meet and overnight letters to be rushed to the post office thirteen miles away.

Delmer quickly learned about television stations, antennas, and towers from the engineer of a local television station who had space to rent and equipment to sell. They went to the mountains together, and he learned what types of equipment were needed to set up a television station and how to do it.

Evelyn faithfully attacked her job of writing letters to anyone and everyone Delmer thought would be interested. With a persistent determination to be optimistic and supportive, she sat before the computer for hours. The telephone bills and postage stamps cost more and more to keep abreast of the mountain of paperwork. A lot of time was spent in prayer.

Oh, dear God, her heart prayed as she sat at the computer. *Whenever someone rejects the idea of a new Christian television station, it seems as if I am the one being rejected. It is Your work, Lord. But there seems to be so few people who are interested.*

"Evelyn, I'll give as much money as Joe[*] gives to start a new television station," confided Peter,[*] a good friend and relative who had come to visit that afternoon.

"Really?" Evelyn looked suprised.

How could he? Joe is much better fixed financially than

---

[*] Names have been changed

Peter, she thought.

"That's because..." Peter flashed his charming smile.

"I know Joe isn't going to give any."

The knife in Evelyn's heart would not go away. Peter's words kept churning through her mind, and that evening, dinner was salted with her tears. She decided they must completely rely on God. Their friends surely weren't much help.

It was then that she claimed Psalm 46:1, "God is our refuge and strength, a very present help in trouble."

CHAPTER 2

Dark clouds poured rain on the lush landscape. The water made little streams across the green lawn and down the driveway before it plunged over the bank, tumbling to the restless creek below. Evelyn clicked on her computer and began writing to her long-time friend Juanita Kretschmar, director of the Evangelistic Van Center in New York City. She concluded the message by saying, "I am sorry not to be able to send any donation for the work there at this time. Since Delmer is so excited about getting good Christian programming on TV here in Grants Pass, that is where our money is going."

She gathered a few pieces of literature that Delmer had written about the possibility of starting a television station and put them in an envelope. *I know Juanita will understand.* She attached a stamp and sealed the envelope. *Dear God.* Evelyn bowed her head. *Please do not let us make a mistake. We only want to serve You, and there are so many needy projects. This TV work seems so...so... overwhelming.*

Pastor Merlin Kretschmar, president of the Greater New York Conference for Seventh-day Adventists, and his wife, Juanita, were visionary people. They had been praying for a radio or TV station for years. When they received Evelyn's letter, they asked Delmer to see what possibilities there were in getting air space in New York City. They already had a TV studio and many programs. What an opportunity to have a TV station of their own!

Delmer went to his computer and started studying FCC reports. He called television stations in New York City. He spent hours looking for air space for a TV station he hoped to start in the city of New York. He booked a flight and also found that he had enough free air miles available so Evelyn could go with him. Now they were actually on their way to New York City. But why hadn't they received a report back from the study about the availability of air space there? Delmer had called Washington, DC, repeatedly, and he always received the same answer. "We will be getting a report to you in a few days."

"I feel silly going to New York to see about setting up a TV station, when we do not even know if there is air space." Evelyn was concerned.

"Don't worry." Delmer looked out the window and watched the bright sunlight shimmering on the white clouds below. "Those reports don't always find everything. Even if they think there is no available space, what of it? If God wants a special TV station in New York, there will be one."

"Oh, I know," she said, while thinking, *Delmer doesn't expect anything to stop him from going forward on this project.* She laid her head back on the seat and closed her eyes.

They had expected to land at John F. Kennedy International Airport, but because of the storms, they had been rerouted many miles away to an airport in New Jersey.

"You made it." Juanita was standing among dozens of people waiting for the passengers who were disembarking from the plane. "This is Charles." She introduced the tall young man at her side. "He knows the way over here better than I do, and I didn't want to get lost. Marilyn, my secretary, is in the car. We couldn't find a good place to park, so she stayed with the car in case it has to be moved."

"I am so sorry you had to come so far and so late at night." Evelyn apologized to Juanita, as Charles and Delmer went to get the luggage.

"No problem." Juanita paused as the two of them stood watching the multitude of people rushing by. "That is no problem, but I must tell you, Evelyn, I have some bad news."

The loaded car inched its way through the heavy traffic, while Juanita shared the news with Delmer and Evelyn. "Sacks-Freeman Associates called and said there is no air space available in this New York area. I knew you couldn't get the money back from the airlines for your tickets, so I thought you might as well use them. I wanted you to see how things have changed since the last time you were here, anyway."

While the car slowly moved along in bumper-to-bumper traffic, Delmer made plans about what he should do. He would go to Washington, DC; he would see more people; he would check more data. His unstoppable enthusiasm to continue moving forward to start a TV station for the E-Van-gelism Center was still there.

CHAPTER 3

Don't people ever sleep around here? It was close to midnight, but the six-lane highway was a solid line of cars as far as one could see. Marilyn, the driver, turned from the main freeway and came down the road to the elegant, old colonial-style mansion used as the E-Van-gelism Center headquarters. They stopped in front of the large brick building called "The Van Center" or "Center."

As Delmer and Charles unloaded the luggage from the trunk of the car, Juanita moved to the driver's seat. "I hope you can get some good rest." She started the car and left for her home about six miles away.

The men carried the luggage through the large lobby and up the wide, curved stairway of the Center to the room on the second floor where Delmer and Evelyn would be staying.

The next morning, seven o'clock came early. After getting ready, they headed toward the dining area where a hot breakfast awaited them and the staff members who lived at the Center.

At eight o'clock, they gathered in the worship room for song, prayer, and a special devotional service. Many of the people gathered there that morning would be going out to claim people for the Lord from Satan's territory. They did not plan to try it on their own.

Delmer set himself up in an office where he could make phone calls and work on the details for a TV frequency.

Excitement filled Evelyn's heart when Juanita asked if

she would like to go out in one of the vans with a couple of the young people who lived at the Center—Jeff would be taking blood pressures, and Lorie would be the receptionist.

It was the Christmas season, and the crisp morning air made their breath hang in space like little clouds of smoke. Evelyn shivered as she, along with Jeff and Lorie, climbed into the big van and again bowed their heads while Lorie asked God for guidance and protection for the day. Jeff then checked to see if the boxes of literature, books, and a few Bibles were securely stored in place. Soon they were slowly winding their way through the traffic toward the great metropolitan area.

Evelyn sat by the window, enjoying the sights as the van gradually moved along. She picked up her camera and took some pictures. Unexpectedly, Jeff changed lanes on a four-lane bridge and came to a complete stop. Cars went speeding around them. He grabbed a *Signs of the Times* and headed for the side door. He stood there a minute as the cars whizzed by, and then, seeing a break in the traffic, opened the door and was gone!

"Those people have been sitting in their stalled car for hours." Jeff was heading the van back into the line of traffic. "No one has stopped to help them. I told them that as soon as we got to our stop and I could find a phone, I would call for help. They really appreciated it and seemed glad to get the literature too. It will give them something to read while they wait."

"That was fast maneuvering of this big bus. How did you think so quickly?" Evelyn was amazed.

"Oh, I have passed so many people who needed help in the past." Jeff continued concentrating on his driving. "I ask God to help me think rapidly enough so I can help people who need it before whizzing by."

Crowded houses sat pressed together, and the tall buildings reached for the sky. Roaring motors and honking horns tried to drown out Evelyn's thoughts. *Was that siren a police car or an ambulance?* Jeff and Lorie took it all in stride. This was a different world from Evelyn's mountain home in Oregon.

The van stopped at the designated place for the day, and the people began lining up outside. Jeff arranged the blood pressure room, and Lorie set up the reception area. There was a stack of *Signs of the Times* and also a literature rack in the reception area. Before the door opened to welcome the people in, they bowed their heads and sent another prayer up to heaven, asking God's presence to fill the place and that God would bring the right people to the van that day.

Amid the Christmas rush, Evelyn handed out beautiful new *Signs of the Times* magazines. Some individuals shook their heads, refusing the gift, but most seemed pleased to get the magazines. After about half an hour, she climbed back into the van out of the icy air that was nipping at her toes and fingers.

Michael, a minister who lived in the area, came into the van bundled up in a heavy coat, cap, and gloves. He casually visited with everyone there. Anyone seeming interested, he invited to a fellowship meeting at his home on Saturday afternoon. He then looked at his watch. "I had better get to passing out this literature."

Two and a half hours later, Pastor Michael came into the waiting room and sat down. "They are all gone. I knew it would not take long to give out that stack of *Signs of the Times* magazines."

Bright lights challenged the darkness trying to cover the

city. They must head home. A man was talking with Pastor Michael, and although the strong odor of alcohol filled the little room, he seemed interested in spiritual things and wanted to learn more. Pastor Michael invited him to come to his home Saturday afternoon, and the man said he would be there. The man started out the door, but turned and came back.

"I would really like to bring my wife and kids." He spoke quietly with pleading eyes. He was assured the whole family was welcome. The man beamed. "I will see you Saturday afternoon for sure."

It was late by this time. Jeff knew he would be driving in rush-hour traffic.

CHAPTER 4

Things were quickly put away, and Jeff slowly eased the big van out into the ever-present traffic.

"I don't like leaving so late." He was now moving along with the swarming vehicles. "It takes twice as long to get anywhere in this congestion." Then he saw a stalled car. Traffic moved into the other lanes to get around the automobile. Jeff squeezed the van between the moving vehicles and stopped by the car. Several tired, frustrated people sat in the crowded auto. They had waited for hours hoping someone would stop and help them.

"Those people had about given up thinking anyone would stop." Jeff climbed back into the van. "I don't know why no one will help. All you have to do is make a phone call. They belong to AAA so help should soon be on the way. I told them I would call as soon as we got back to the Center."

By the time the van pulled up to the parking lot in front of the big brick building and they had climbed the stairs to their rooms, it was almost time for prayer meeting. Most of the staff members were already on their way to the worship area. Delmer had finished his work for the day, so he and Evelyn picked up their Bibles and followed the others.

Pastor Merlin Kretschmar was in charge of the prayer meeting that evening, and after the song service and prayer, each person had the opportunity to read three or four verses from Scripture.

The pastor had chosen verses from 1 and 2 Chronicles and

also from 1 Kings. They told how God had chosen Solomon, before his birth, to do a special work for Him. The glorious beginning of Solomon's reign as king was never equaled. The story didn't stop there, and each person read more verses. Solomon stopped obeying God, and the Bible told the sad story of his disobedience. Yes, Solomon did repent; however, we can only imagine what the difference would have been if Solomon had continued to humbly obey his God.

"What a prayer meeting!" Delmer and Evelyn had reached their room. "That was so simple and yet so powerful. Do you get the feeling with so much prayer going on around here that we are walking on holy ground? I think that is the reason God is performing so many miracles," Evelyn said.

"Merlin needed to give a prayer meeting like that so that no one will take credit himself. It is God making the program a success. I was reading in *Evangelism* somewhere—let me see where I marked it." Evelyn picked up the book by Ellen White that lay on the table. "Oh, yes, here it is on page 333. 'The Lord would do great things for the workers, but their hearts are not humble. Should the Lord work in them, they would become lifted up, filled with self-esteem and...'" She switched off the light. It had been a long day. What would they find out tomorrow?

CHAPTER 5

Shafts of light shot higher and higher into the eastern sky the next morning. Charles, the young man living at the Van Center whom Delmer and Evelyn had met at the airport, scraped ice from the windshield of the car he was warming up. The cold was cruel, but the car felt warm and comfortable inside.

"Try to work it into the schedule so we can see the Capitol." Evelyn was trying not to miss anything as they sped down the road toward Washington, DC. "It is something I have wanted to see all of my life."

Charles and Delmer visited the offices of many of the people Delmer had already talked with on the telephone while still in Oregon. Evelyn stayed in the car, petitioning God for His direction and guidance, and if it was His will, they would be able to find air space for a television station for the Van Center.

Darkness was closing in by the time Delmer finally found the place for his last appointment. Charles and Evelyn used the time to dash through a downpour of rain to a fast-food restaurant to grab something to ease the hunger pains. The water had begun coming down in sheets, and the curb drains were sluggish, causing the sides of the pavement to turn into raging little creeks.

The rain, pouring through the darkness, soaked Delmer's clothes as he raced back to the car. He shielded piles of computer printouts under his coat. The verdict: no air space available that would not interfere with another station.

Charles started the engine of the little brown car as he queried, "Where to now?"

"We better get back to New York," Delmer said to Charles, as he handed Evelyn a large stack of papers—reports on television frequencies in New York City. She laid them on the seat beside her, and Charles drove the car through a downpour of rain back to the Van Center.

Friday morning after worship, Evelyn met Walter, one of the van drivers who also took blood pressures. They were going on one of the big vans to meet whomever the Lord would bring to them. Today she would get to be a receptionist. She bowed her head, and Walter asked for God to be in charge of their day before he guided the big motor vehicle out onto the busy street.

"This is just what I told Juanita I didn't want to do." Walter skillfully drove down the crowded streets. "I told her I didn't plan on driving one of these big vans here in New York City, but as you can see, it is what needed to be done, so I am doing it."

"You surely know how to get around in this jam-packed traffic."

"I have had lots of practice." Walter smiled and then began sharing some of the experiences he had enjoyed since coming to work at the Van Center. She listened with rapt attention.

These stories should go in the Mission Magazines. People need to know what God is doing! Evelyn thought.

Walter eased the van to the side of the street where they would be working that day. Again they bowed their heads in prayer. He got the equipment in order and showed her how to set up the reception area. He then showed her how the health applications should be filled out, fixed the steps, and set up the sign.

"If someone seems to be having trouble filling out the application, be sure to help them." Walter checked the literature rack. "Sometimes a person cannot read or write. Then you just fill in the answers for them. Here are some Spanish applications. Some of the people who come on the van are more comfortable with the Spanish language." He opened the door, and they were ready for business.

"I came in to get my blood pressure taken—not fill out a form." The well-dressed man glared at Evelyn when she tried to hand him an application form.

Now what was she to do? How could she send him in to get his blood pressure taken without the papers filled out? Walter came into the reception area, picked up an application, and said, "Well, my friend, we will need one of these filled out before we take your blood pressure."

"I am not giving my name or address to anyone."

"That is fine." Walter spoke in his kind, professional way. "But we do need to know your health history, so we can make more accurate recommendations." He proceeded to go though the questions on the application with the man, getting information on his health history and habits. "Do you smoke? How much? How many glasses of water do you drink a day?" So many people didn't drink water. Coffee? Yes. Tea or soft drinks? Yes. But water? No.

The two men then stepped into the little room where Walter took his blood pressure, talked about good health habits, and offered him health-related literature.

Evelyn was too busy working with other people to know what Walter and the man said, but she did notice he smiled at her when he left the reception area. Walter told her later that the man had put ten dollars into the little donation box sitting on the table.

While one lady sat waiting her turn, Evelyn noticed that she kept glancing at the rack that said "free literature." Since the lady seemed interested but did not venture to take anything, Evelyn walked to the rack, picked up a *Listen* magazine, and handed it to her. She took it so eagerly that Evelyn picked up a *Signs of the Times* and also handed it to the lady saying, "I think you would enjoy this magazine."

"Oh, thank you." The lady accepted the magazine but started to return the *Listen* magazine to the rack.

"You may have them both if you like." Evelyn smiled. The lady gave her an appreciative smile and carefully placed the literature in her shopping bag. Suddenly another article titled "What is it Like to Die?" caught her eye. Immediately, she exclaimed, "I don't want to die! Oh, I don't want to die!"

"But you might like to read the article." Evelyn took the magazine from the rack along with several pamphlets and handed them to the lady. The lady eagerly took the literature, held it to her heart, and whispered, "I won't be lonely tonight with all of this to read."

"We close early on Friday." Walter began putting things away. Evelyn hurriedly arranged the reception area so that it was ready to travel. Then she had the privilege of listening to mission stories from the city of New York as they traveled back to the Van Center.

Thank you, God. She breathed a prayer as she hurried up the stairs to her room. *Thank you for letting us be here for a whole week. Truly this is holy ground for You are here.*

Vespers was held at the Kretschmar's home every Friday evening and was a delightful place to go for fellowship and worship. Marilyn had invited Delmer and Evelyn to ride to vespers with her.

CHAPTER 6

The Kretschmar home overflowed with guests by the time Marilyn, Delmer, and Evelyn arrived. A couple of young people got up from the couch where they had been sitting and offered them a place to sit. Then these two young people squeezed into a spot on the floor among the many other young people sitting on pillows or just the carpet. Juanita was at the piano, and each person chose a song that spoke the feelings of his or her heart.

Evelyn flipped through the song book. What should she choose? "Praise Him! Praise Him!" That sounded like a good one, but no. "Nearer, Still Nearer" expressed the way she was feeling tonight. She finally chose the song "Trust and Obey." She joined in the singing as one person after another announced the next song to be sung. The words they were singing really were expressing the emotions of the different people there! She felt she could identify with each song and also with the one who had chosen it. One could feel a great fellowship singing together in this manner.

It was nearly Evelyn's turn when the girl sitting next to her on the couch chose the one Evelyn wanted. "Trust and Obey." Now Evelyn quickly flipped through the song book to find another song that expressed the way she felt. However, under the pressure of time, she could not figure out what she wanted, and when it was her turn to decide the next song to be sung, she chose the first one the book opened to. *Anyway they are all good*, she thought. After a short study, praise, and prayer, the meeting came to a close.

The next morning Delmer and Evelyn were up early so they would be ready to go when Merlin and Juanita came by to take them to church. The staff members went to different churches all over the city, filling the needs of many congregations. In the afternoon, there was also another church service in the worship room at the Van Center.

This Sabbath, Merlin preached in a Spanish-speaking church. It was a high day for the congregation. Before they entered the sanctuary, Juanita whispered to Delmer and Evelyn, "Just say, 'Feliz Sabado' when you meet the people."

During the church service, Juanita translated the Spanish sermon into English for them.

"I was going to tell you to relax and enjoy the sermon," Evelyn said after the meeting, a wonderful fellowship luncheon, and visiting. She and Delmer were getting into the car with the Kretschmars. "I am glad I didn't. We would not have wanted to miss that talk for anything."

The Van Ministry in New York City had been a faith ministry from the very beginning as the Kretschmars followed God's leading. God rewarded this faith. When people asked how money was raised for such an undertaking, the answer always was: "through prayer."

When Pastor Merlin Kretschmar was called to New York to be head of a department there, he and Juanita looked down as the plane circled the great city and wondered, "How can we reach these people?"

There wasn't a lot of money for a big campaign. You cannot knock on doors unless you want to talk to the armed guard. You have to know someone in the building in order to even get into the huge apartment houses. Merlin and Juanita spent a lot of time praying about it. How did God want to reach these people of His?

"Trust in the Lord with all your heart, and lean not on your own understanding; In all your ways acknowledge Him, and He shall direct your paths." Proverbs 3:5-6 meant a lot to them as they prayed that God would show them how to get in contact with the right people.

Delmer and Evelyn never got tired of hearing the stories of how the Van Center work was started and went forward as the Kretschmars stepped out in faith to follow God's leading. Evelyn decided some of these mission stories must be written down so they would not be forgotten.

Later, back in Oregon, she went to her computer and wrote the following stories, which you can read in the next five chapters of this book. These mission stories remind us again how closely God will work with His children when they are willing to go forward, while completely trusting in Him.

CHAPTER 7

On every corner Merlin and Juanita came to there were masses of people. Juanita would think, "But Lord, you do not see a mass of people. You see individuals. You know every situation about every person, and You love them."

God miraculously helped get the first van, which started the Van Ministry. The conference didn't have any money, but the Kretschmars kept praying. Friends and relatives sent donations, and in about nine month's time they had collected six thousand dollars. Merlin searched every used-van lot on Long Island, and they both kept praying. About all that was available were rusted-out bread trucks. They kept on praying.

One day the Lord brought their attention to a gorgeous van already set up with two rooms so that people could come into the waiting-room area and then go into another room to have their blood pressure taken.

This van had been driven only 4,000 miles and was all aluminum. The people who had it, said when new, this van cost forty thousand dollars, but since it was used, they could let the Kretschmars have it for just thirty-two thousand dollars.

It had taken nine months to raise six thousand dollars. Based on that timeframe, Juanita figured that it would take five years to obtain thirty-two thousand dollars. She got up to leave, and as she was walking away, the man asked, "What is the matter?"

In the course of the conversation, this man began telling them the interesting story about his van, but all Juanita could think of was, *Why are we wasting time here? We have no time. There is no way. We can't afford it.*

He was telling this long, involved story about how it happened to be available, and at the end he said, "By the way, what did you people want it for?"

Merlin had also stood to leave. "We thought we would like to do a service for the community and take blood pressures around the area in the city."

The man became very excited. His wife worked with the heart association. Well, maybe he would see if they could do something special. No one evidently wanted this van, which was custom-made for someone who had traded it back.

He added up on his calculator what it would take just to get their money out of it. It had been used for only one year. When he finished, he said, "I will tell you what; if we would repaint and letter it to your specifications and get it tuned up, what would you say if we charged you eight thousand dollars?"

The conference had said, "We don't have any money. Don't ask us for any."

However, Juanita heard her husband say, "We will take it. Don't do anything else with it between now and five o'clock. I will get a check to you that will be in our conference's name."

Juanita was pretty quiet as she walked to the car. Finally she asked Merlin, "Where are you going to get the other two thousand dollars?"

"Oh, I thought I had told you." He looked at her and smiled. "You know how we have been asking for money from everybody everywhere? Would you believe that just last night I received word from the union that the GC Inter City had voted two thousand dollars for some kind of medical outreach in New York City?"

The Kretschmars purchased the van and took it out on the streets, wondering if people would come in. They prayed for the Holy Spirit to bless, and the people started coming. Many individuals wanted their blood pressure checked, and the Lord kept sending more and more people.

Joe, Merlin and Juanita's oldest son, drove the van that first summer. In the fall, they received allocation funds and were able to hire a driver to work full time. Later, friends donated a couple of used vans, and people started volunteering to help.

They—the Kretschmars, the volunteers, and others who made up the staff—prayed for the Holy Spirit. They were out on the street corners taking blood pressures, but they were praying that the Lord would bring people into the vans who needed to know that He loved them.

How would taking people's blood pressure let people know that God loves them? The staff members were there, and the Lord sent those who needed something special from Him to the vans. The staff members were giving blood pressure checks; but if the person needed something more, the volunteers were praying for the Holy Spirit to help them have their minds and their mouths open.

The vans were sent out with a lot of prayer as they went into the different communities. And the people came. They filled out the forms and accepted the additional material. The Kretschmars decided they would like to give the people something to read, so friends sent their old magazines and books. They were praying, and the people kept coming to the vans. The people literally grabbed anything they could get—Bibles, *Steps to Christ, The Great Controversy, Signs of the Times*. You name it—if it was there, they took it.

It was sobering to realize how interested the people were.

Juanita said there were some people who came on the vans who said, "You know, I was on the way to the river to commit suicide, and I saw the van…"

CHAPTER 8

"I was on my way to the river to commit suicide, and I saw the van. Somehow I was impressed if someone inside the van would smile at me, I would know that there was still reason to be alive today."

It was clear that God put the vans where He wanted them to save lives. Merlin and Juanita along with the rest of the staff just kept praying. "Lord, send us the people." They were there to take blood pressures, and people just kept coming.

Free public service advertisements were broadcast on radio and television, telling people where to call to find out where the vans would be. Sometimes the people calling in to find out where the blood pressure vans were going to park started unburdening themselves of whatever problem was bothering them. Sooner or later one of the staff—whoever happened to answer the phone at that particular time—said, "Would you like me to pray with you?"

Juanita said, "The word of mouth had gone around that when the phone rang, we prayed with people."

Since there were so many people who wanted information about how to stop smoking, Juanita decided they needed to have more material on the subject. They got a little old printing press and started printing this material, and the people started taking it. So many people seemed to be interested in material on nutrition that they started printing that, too.

There were other people who were asking for something spiritual. Juanita had some Bible lessons that she had written, so she thought that she would just offer these to the people. From the day they began offering the people this Bible series, one out of every three people who came on the van said, "Yes, I would like to have that."

These were the results of praying and having people come on the van to have their blood pressure checked. There were no plans to have a Bible school, but before long the staff members were mailing two thousand Bible lessons out every week. They did not even have a typewriter to start with. The upstairs hallway of the Kretschmar's home became the space for the office work, and there wasn't much room for that or for anything else. They prayed as the mail went out, and they prayed as the mail came in.

Juanita said, "If you are going to do anything for the Lord—anything God calls you to do—**you** are not doing it. The **Holy Spirit** causes the people to ask for something."

God miraculously opened up a nice place with plenty of room where the staff could go and do the work that needed to be done. They continued meeting people in the vans out on the streets, working with them and taking blood pressures.

One day WNBC-TV invited the Kretschmars into their Manhattan offices. WNBC-TV and the National Health Screening Council met with them. The network director of community affairs and the New York City director of city affairs were there. They said, "We have been observing your church and your work. There is no other organization as close to the people as you are. For the last two years, we have been sponsoring a week-long health fair in the tri-state area. We would like you to coordinate this next year's project for New York, New Jersey, and Connecticut. You'll be coordinating about 20,000 volunteers and 700 or 800 organizations that will be helping in the health fair."

The Kretschmars went home and prayed about it. It was an experience that would bring the church into prominence. People all over would be watching what was going on and would be aware of Seventh-day Adventists.

Prayerfully they agreed to accept the responsibility of co-ordinating the health fair. The whole issue grew bigger each day. It was running on prayer, and they kept wondering what they were doing and how to keep going.

After the health fair was over, and they all collapsed for awhile, they began looking at the registration forms of the people who had come to the health fair follow-up.

They noticed that many people had indicated on the forms that they wanted information on how to handle stress. The Van Center outreach could not afford to buy some of the already printed material, so Juanita decided to write some Bible study guides on how to handle stress and just mail them to those people who had come to the health fair follow-up.

As fast as she wrote a guide, it was printed. One day as she was writing the second or third guide, Donna, one of the staff nurses and also a van driver, came in. "Juanita, what are you doing?"

"I am writing some Bible guides for handling stress to send to the people who came to the health fair earlier this year."

"Oh." She looked at the Bible guides. "We are going to get to use them on the vans aren't we?"

"No. We already have the other Bible studies that we use. You know one out of every three who come on the vans take them."

"But they need these out on the vans."

"Donna, don't rock the boat. Everything is going very nicely. We are doing fine."

"Oh, please."

"Donna, don't pester. Everything is so organized. We don't want to get our lives uprooted."

"Please. I won't tell anyone. Please let me just try it."

"If one person finds out that you are doing it, everyone will probably want to do it; and it will be a big problem."

"I won't tell a soul. Not even the person out in the waiting room will know that I am giving out the Bible guides. Instead of offering the other Bible guides, I will offer these."

"Alright, take the first one with you, and you can try it tomorrow."

Donna came back the next day and closed the door behind her. "Guess what, Juanita. One hundred percent of the people wanted them."

"Did you tell them they were spiritual?"

On the vans, everyone is supposed to always be up front, hiding nothing. Seventh-day Adventist is written in big letters across the vans. There are a lot of people who are agnostics and atheists who come on the vans.

"You did tell the people that this is spiritual material didn't you?"

"Oh, I guess I didn't. I guess I just told them it was for stress."

"So who in New York wouldn't take material on stress? It doesn't count."

"Can I do it tomorrow? Let me just try it tomorrow."

"Alright."

She came back the next day and closed the door behind her for their big secret. "Guess what. I told everybody it was spiritual material on how to handle stress, and 90 percent of the people wanted it."

"Where were you today, Donna?"

"Coop City."

Everybody knows that Coop City is mostly Jewish. "Donna, you did tell them it was Judeo-Christian biblical guidelines of course, didn't you?"

"No. I just said spiritual."

"That doesn't count. Not that we don't want the people to take them. But you have to let them know, and if they make the choice to take them, fine."

"Oh, well. Let me try again tomorrow."

"Alright; try tomorrow."

She came back the next day, and closing the door behind her, said, "Juanita, I don't know what to do. I told the people they were spiritual. I told them they were biblical. I told them they were Judeo Christian. I think that 65 or 70 percent of the people still wanted them. What shall we do now?"

Juanita looked at her, and she looked at Juanita. They couldn't think of anything else to keep the people from taking the new Bible studies!

CHAPTER 9

Juanita was writing *Power to Cope Guide No. 4* when the following incident happened. She had already finished the three previous guides and was now working on the next edition.

Power to Cope Guide No. 1 talked about the fact that if you have an attitude of gratitude it helps you get through stress much easier than if you do not. Of course, all of these studies bring out the importance of exercise, fresh air, and all the natural health laws. Still, having an attitude of gratitude goes a long way in overcoming stress. For a good demonstration of the attitude of gratitude, who would be better than someone who was spending most of his time running for his life from his father-in-law? David! So it presented a Bible story. That made the transition from medical information to biblical information, and it included some Bible promises.

The second guide dealt with the stress of guilt. A lot of people have different types of stress, but one cause of stress is a sense of guilt. There is only one thing to do with guilt—take it to Jesus and receive forgiveness, which is free.

Power to Cope Guide No. 3 answered the questions: If God has forgiven and taken all the guilt of my sin, then why is my mind such a battlefield? Why isn't everything great now? Why do I have to go through so much turmoil? This guide dealt with the battle going on between two supernatural powers. Ultimately Christ is the victor over Satan, but in this world there is still a supernatural battle going on for control.

Power to Cope Guide No. 4 pointed out the fact that we are free. So many people have a lot of stress because they see innocent people suffer. They see evil doers who are prospering. They see so much abuse and so much that is unfair. That provokes stress and is a real issue in the whole problem of inner stress. So that guide dealt with the passages of scripture that tell us: Fret not yourself because of evil doers (Psalm 37 and Proverbs 24:19) because God is still in control. You are free to forgive. Leave the punishing to God. He is going to address these issues. You don't have to feel you have to punish people. You are free to forgive and leave their case with God. You are free to accept God's love and forgiveness.

On Tuesday morning Juanita finished writing the fourth guide, and in the afternoon she was writing the month's newsletter about experiences on the vans. She was home writing when she received a phone call from a lady who is a lawyer in the United Nations for her country's government (not the USA). Juanita had introduced this lady to Jesus, and she had accepted Him. The two women now enjoyed a good friendship. This lady really loved God. She loved God before she ever met Jesus, and meeting Jesus was like icing on the cake—just wonderful. She didn't have a Bible in her own language so she didn't know much about Him except as Juanita shared with her.

As they were chatting along, the lady said, "By the way, Juanita, are you wondering why I am calling in the middle of the day? I wanted to tell you I got struck by a hit-and-run driver last Friday night, and I am home with a bruised leg." Juanita told her how sorry she was about that, and the lady said, "You know, it was so awful. Here I am a lawyer, and I did not even get his license number.

"Let me tell you why I am calling you—because of something really strange. Before the accident, as I was getting ready to cross the street, all of a sudden some big man just kind of pressed against me. I turned to see who would do that to me, and as I turned, I saw this car bearing down upon me. I jumped back, and it caught me on the leg. Do you realize if I hadn't turned at that moment and seen the car, I would have been run over and killed? As it was, the car only got my leg, and it didn't break any bones—just bruises."

She continued, "Now I have to tell you why I am calling. When I turned and looked to see who the man was who had pressed against me, why Juanita, there was nobody there. What was that?"

Juanita told her about guardian angels. Then this lady exclaimed, "Oh, I thought Jesus would do something like that!"

They prayed together and then got off the phone. Juanita went on writing, telling the lady's story in the letter. As she ended the letter, she called to see if this lady would give her permission to tell her story if Juanita didn't tell who she was. Juanita also wanted to be sure that she had the story right.

Juanita called around eight o'clock that evening. When the lady picked up the phone and heard Juanita's voice she exclaimed, "Oh, Juanita, I want to talk to you again! I know how busy you are, and I hate to take your time, but I need to talk to you."

"Oh, wonderful," Juanita answered. "And I need to talk with you."

"You tell me first."

Juanita read to her what she had written in the letter and asked her permission to use it. She said, "Oh, it is all correct. Fine. Use it."

"Now tell me why you wanted to call me again." Juanita

waited.

The lady paused a moment. "You know, after I finished talking on the phone today, I stayed in prayer another two or three hours, because I was still rather upset about the fact that the driver got away. As I prayed, God spoke to me, and He gave me a message. He said it was for you, and I was to tell you.

"God said, 'Here is the message: You should not fret about people who are evil doers. You should realize that God is in control and that they will be punished in His way and in His own time, but that you are free to forgive, by His Holy Spirit's power.' Then He told me, 'You are to tell Juanita about it because she will know how to let everybody know.'"

As Juanita listened she had chills going up and down her spine. It was the exact message found in *Power to Cope Guide No. 4* that she had just finished writing that morning. The lady had repeated to Juanita almost word for word the entire message of that Bible lesson!

"Now, Juanita, did you get all of that?" She waited.

Juanita said, "Uh, huh."

"You are sure?"

"Yes, I already have it." (She didn't understand what Juanita meant.)

"I am glad you do. I guess I'm free to forgive whomever that was who hit me."

They prayed and got off the phone. A couple of weeks later this lady came by Juanita's house. *Power to Cope Guide No. 4* had been printed by then.

"I have something to show you." Juanita handed the lady *Power to Cope Guide No. 4.*

She began reading. "Oh right! That is just right. You got that just right! Do you take shorthand, Juanita? That is just exactly what He said."

"No, that was already written before you ever called me."

God is ready to confirm His message to us, and He will let us know what He wishes to be done. Juanita had no idea how much God wanted that message to go out to everyone. When there was such a positive response, all of the van drivers were given permission to offer the *Power to Cope* Bible lessons to everyone who came on the vans.

Within two or three weeks, a man from Ohio walked into their office. He had a computer under his arm and said, "I am impressed by God that you people need a computer."

"We do?"

"Yes."

What God knew, and they didn't, was that the Bible school was about to double. Instead of mailing 2,000 a week, they began mailing about 4,000 lessons or more. We are talking about a lot of blessings—blessings that they did not have room to receive, and by the following year, they were in the middle of another problem.

The problem was the fact that during that first year, forty thousand people had asked for *Power to Cope* Bible guides for handling stress. That is a huge load of printing, mailing, and all sorts of things. They had continued to move forward on faith through this mission project, and Juanita thought she had a lot of faith by now.

"Have you ever had the mistaken idea that God's work depends on you?" Juanita asked the question, and then said, "Somehow in my mind I guess I was falling for the trap that my newsletters were causing people to give donations, or at least, reminding them to. In July I didn't have time to get the newsletter out. My husband had become the conference president a few years before, and I was trying to fill many other roles. We had a staff of about thirty people by then, and we hadn't printed a newsletter that month.

"One Friday in August, the bookkeeper said, 'Juanita, by my figures, next week we are going to need five thousand more dollars than we have, in order to meet our bills.'

"I thought, 'I didn't get that newsletter out! I didn't have time, God. You know that I didn't have time.'

"The next morning in my personal devotions I was feeling mad at God just a little. I felt like, 'Why do I have to work so much harder than anybody else? Why, God? Why don't I get to go to church and enjoy Sabbath morning? Why do I have to feel a guilt trip, God? Anyone else can go and worship and be at peace, and I have to sit here feeling nervous and worried because where is the five thousand dollars coming from? I know, God, that I shouldn't be angry, but, God, what are we going to do? I didn't get that newsletter out.'"

CHAPTER 10

Juanita was still up tight as she left her devotions and headed out to the car to go with her husband to church. There was just one letter in the mail, and it was from some people they had gone to school with at Walla Walla. These people had sent maybe twenty-five or fifty dollars up to that time—Juanita knew they lived on a tight budget. She decided if she opened this letter she would read news from this nice Christian family. So on the way to church, she opened the envelope and pulled out their letter. A check fell out, but she did not bother to look at it and started reading. It was only a couple of paragraphs long. It started with the usual, "How are you? I hope things are going fine." The note talked about their family and in conclusion said simply, "We were impressed you needed some help. Enclosed is a check. Love..."

Juanita picked up the check, and it was for **five thousand dollars**!! "Oh, God!" Juanita almost wept, "Not them to teach me that it is not up to me, but it is up to You." She couldn't believe how clear God had been!

The next month, things were a little rougher, because by this time, they had used up any and all of their resources. The regular funds coming in were just barely enough to keep the mailings going. This was the year with all the influx of interest in *Power to Cope*.

Juanita said, "I had figured out something. I had learned this thing is no longer up to me. After what had happened with the five thousand dollars, I knew it wasn't my problem any longer." In September, the man who was keeping books called Juanita into his office and said, "Juanita, I have news for you. By my figures, if we are going to meet all the bills next week that we regularly have every month—electricity, water, stipends, mailing, etc.—we are twelve thousand dollars short of what we need with all of these expenses. So I was wondering what you are going to do about all of this."

"Why don't we have a word of prayer?" Juanita answered and knelt down.

"Juanita, you don't seem to understand! We need twelve thousand dollars next week!"

"It is God's fault that we have this problem with all of these blessings. If He wants to bless, He will have to be responsible for it. So do you want to pray with me about it or not?"

This man was a retired business man who had come to help. He said, "Lady, I am really serious! It looks like we are *short* twelve thousand dollars!!"

"I am really serious, too. Do you want to pray with me?" Juanita asked.

"I am not used to doing business like this."

"It is the only way I know how to do business around here," Juanita answered.

They knelt and prayed. When they got up, he asked, "What are you going to do about the twelve thousand dollars?"

"I don't know. We JUST asked God. Now we will have to see what God is going to do."

The next day Juanita was home writing the newsletter. Merlin called from the conference office. "Do you remember last year when we were down in Dallas at the General Conference session? Do you remember the couple who came to the van and said that their dad had worked in New York in the 1930s and he had left a trust fund and if there was money left in it, they wanted it to go for the medical van program?"

"Yes, but when we got back, no one could find any trace of the money."

"That's right, except that someone was cleaning out some old musty file boxes up in the attic today. As they were going through these old boxes, they found an old bank book. Would you believe there is some money left in it? And it's from the people we met last year. If you can get a statement in writing from those people, as the heirs in the family, saying it should go for this…"

Juanita phoned the people long distance. They said, "Fine," and promised to send a statement by overnight mail.

Juanita had to leave right away because a friend, Dr. Gardner, and she were holding a lifestyle seminar in the Bronx that day. Around ten o' clock that evening on the way home, Juanita went by the Van Center to drop off the staff members who were with her. The bookkeeper was standing in the doorway.

Juanita thought, *I must talk to him.*

She got out of the car, and heard him ask, "Sister Kretschmar, is it too late to talk with you now?"

"No. I need to talk with you anyway."

He said, "I have some bad news."

Juanita responded, "Okay, I have some good news."

"Could we step back to my office?" She followed him back to his office and asked, "Should we have a word of prayer before we get started?"

"Sure," he answered.

They knelt and said a brief prayer, and then they sat down and Juanita asked, "Well, who should be first?"

"My news is bad news," he responded.

"Since my news is good news, why don't you let me tell you first?" She told him the story of how *this day* that bankbook had been found—and the heirs were sending authorization to have the funds released the next day (tomorrow). "Do you know how much was in that account?" Juanita asked.

"How much was in it?"

"Fourteen thousand dollars."

He sat there for awhile. His nose was twitching a bit.

"I just thought you would want to know that the bad news was that I had calculated wrong yesterday. We are not twelve thousand dollars short. We are fourteen thousand dollars short."

"Do you suppose we should kneel down and thank Him?" Juanita pointed upwards.

"I am not used to doing business like this." The man spoke slowly.

"It's the only way I know how to do business around here," she told him. So they knelt and thanked God together.

October came and there was *nothing* left. We are talking about lots of money not available. They had used up *every source* they had. They would be lucky to finish mailing out all of the rest of the lessons for the rest of the year if they closed down.

Juanita called the staff together for a meeting and told them, "I just wanted you to know that evidently God wants us to stop our ministry, because there are no more funds for us to keep up with the demands that we have. I have total faith in God that, this is His ministry, and so it is alright with me if He closes it. This is His work, and if He chooses to close it, that is fine." Juanita gave them a little pep talk, and then continued, "If any of you want to take the day off and go job hunting, I give you permission, because I know some of you have some personal responsibilities that must be met. So feel free to take the day off."

They looked at Juanita and grinned. Some said, "You are joking, Juanita, aren't you?"

"I am not joking."

"Oh, sure you are. If God wanted us to close, why would He be blessing us so much?"

"I am really not joking. I really believe that some of you should go job hunting—especially those who have rent to pay and children to keep in church school."

"No, we will pray, and God will send us the money." Then they prayed, and Juanita prayed with them.

They went to the presses. They went to work to send out the Bible lessons, and they went out on the vans. Everyone went to their jobs as though there was nothing new. Juanita said, "I remember going into my office and kneeling down and crying because of my staff. I have people who have been drug addicts and have seen freedom, alcoholics who have seen freedom, gossipers who have seen freedom—sinners of all types who have had victory when Christ came into their lives.

"I was weeping at the thought that, 'Lord, they really believe that You are going to do something about this. Now God, You and I know this is next to impossible, and Lord, I just don't want these people to lose their faith in You because You choose to close the program. It is alright if You do, but I just don't want them to think that because this prayer isn't answered it means that You don't give victory over sin. Please, God, just protect them when they don't see their prayers answered.'"

Juanita wrote the newsletter for the month. In the newsletter she told stories of that month and mentioned at the end of the newsletter that they would probably be closing, but that would be alright because they had already reached tens of thousands of people, and it was God's work.

CHAPTER 11

Juanita received a phone call a few days later from a lady who lives in the Bronx and had received the newsletter. "Juanita, I want to tell you a story about what happened. A couple days ago your newsletter came. It was about nine thirty in the morning, and I was lying on my couch because I wasn't feeling very well. As I was lying there, I began reading the letter. When I finished, I knelt down by the sofa and held the letter up to God.

"I said, 'God, I think the Kretschmars are discouraged. Maybe they are all discouraged. Now, God, they obviously need money, and if I had fifty dollars, I would give it to them. If they had fifty dollars they could stay open, and I would give it, God, if I just had fifty dollars. You need to give me fifty dollars so I can give it to them, if you will give it to me.'"

She lay back down, and God impressed her to read the letter again. "I read it the second time, and when I finished reading it, I prayed again. I continued praying for the next two or three hours, always asking God for the fifty dollars so you wouldn't have to close."

Around one o'clock that afternoon, she got up and dressed because she was expecting a little piano student. The little girl came in about two o'clock for her piano lesson. As she came in, she handed the lady an envelope.

"What is this?" She took the envelope.

"Mamma said to give it to you."

When she looked into the envelope, she started shaking

because there was a fifty dollar check in it. "Your mother doesn't owe me any money. Here, take it."

"No. Mamma said you are to have it."

"But why?"

"I don't know."

"Isn't Mamma going to pick you up after your piano lesson?"

"Uh, huh."

"Why didn't Mamma give it to me?"

"I don't know."

The lady taught her the piano lesson. After the piano lesson was over, her mother came in. She told her daughter, "Come on, Honey. We have to go."

Mrs. Foster, the piano teacher, stopped the lady. "Here, dear, you don't owe me any money. Here is your money."

The woman again started for the door. "No, I don't want it. Just keep it. That is fine."

"No, really. Keep your money. You don't owe me any money."

"No, no! You keep it! I don't want it!!"

"Why are you giving it to me?"

"It is alright. You just keep it."

"But I want to know. I have a special reason."

"Well, I will tell you some other time. But I am in a hurry." And she literally ran out of the house.

Mrs. Foster was able to speak with this lady, who was a nurse, on the phone the following evening. "You have to tell me why you gave me that check."

The woman hesitated. "I would really rather not. It is a little embarrassing."

"I have to hear the story."

"Well alright—about nine thirty or ten o'clock yesterday morning, I was going about my work, and all of a sudden a voice spoke to me clear as a bell. 'Give Sister Foster fifty dollars.'

"I looked around, and there was not a soul there, so I continued with my work. Pretty soon I heard the voice again, 'Give Sister Foster fifty dollars.' I didn't see anyone. It spoke two or three more times, and finally I answered the voice. 'I don't have fifty dollars.' Again the voice said, 'Give Sister Foster fifty dollars.'

"For the next three or four hours yesterday—every little while this voice would say, 'Give Sister Foster fifty dollars.' I was just ignoring it, but all of a sudden about one o'clock or so, the voice spoke again, but this time it was almost like a threat, **'GIVE SISTER FOSTER FIFTY DOLLARS.'** It was ominous! I just froze and didn't move. I had never heard anything so frightening in my life. Pretty soon the voice spoke again in the same tone, **'GIVE SISTER FOSTER FIFTY DOLLARS.'**

"I tell you, I didn't want to hear the sound of that voice a third time! I went straight over to my desk, got out my checkbook, and wrote a check for fifty dollars. Honey, I don't know what you need fifty dollars for, but I don't care! You can have it. I don't want it."

Sister Foster exclaimed, "That was the time I was praying!" Then, on the phone, Sister Foster told the woman her story of the previous day. That nurse got in her car and drove across the Bronx to where Sister Foster lived.

Sister Foster opened the door. The lady walked into the house and threw herself on the rug in the middle of Sister Foster's living room. "Pray for me. It must have been **God's voice** that I was ignoring!" So Sister Foster got on her knees too and said, "God, You did hear me, didn't You?" And she thanked God for her nurse friend whom God had used to answer her prayer.

God did hear. The fifty dollars was not the only donation received. Incredibly, the Kretschmars were able to pay all the October bills by November 11 and the November bills by December 4. Just to prove how God keeps books, the last day of the year the office was open—in the last mail of the day—there were enough funds to complete and end the year in the black!

This outreach for God became a Bible school that mailed out from four to six thousand Bible lessons and other material each week—until God spoke audibly, saying they should merge all the *Power To Cope* Bible guides into one magazine, which were handed out on the vans and didn't have to be mailed anymore. They had a television program that was aired five or six hours a week free of charge on several stations throughout the New York area. Working with the churches in the city, they began sharing 1,500 to 2,000 meals with hungry people of the city every week.

God had shown them, "You can trust Me for the first two thousand dollars, and you can trust Me for the tens of thousands of dollars. You can trust Me because I love people." There is a God who is alive. There is a God who loves us.

Later, they were given a beautiful van, and with the money received when it was sold, they purchased a four-color printing press. With the four-color printing press, they were able to make the *Power to Cope* lesson guides very attractive. God knew they needed this printing press, for soon after receiving it, The National Laymen's Bible Committee distributed 35,000 *Power to Cope* lesson guides to every thought-leader across America.

Evelyn watched as mission stories seemed to be happening every day they were in New York City. Is it any wonder she longed to be a part of this mission for the Lord as it continued to go *forward* as God led the way?

CHAPTER 12

Sunday morning was bright and cold as Delmer and Evelyn climbed into the big van with Mark, one of the van drivers. He placed a large box of literature behind the front seat, and after a short prayer, they were heading for an old church several miles away. At the church, they helped carry sacks of warm clothes, coats, and a few pillows into the van. Then they carried boxes of several hundred crisp brown bags each filled with two sandwiches and an apple. Next, two men carried a large container of steaming hot soup into the van and placed it in a secure spot. After two of these containers were loaded and well wrapped to stay hot, the crew got into the van and headed across the city to help the needy, hungry street people.

As the big vehicle came to its first stop, Evelyn quickly evaluated the situation. She was glad there were three more men and ladies from the church with them, for fear gripped her heart. People came running from all directions. Two big fellows forced their way through the crowd, up the steps, and into the van. Surely God was speaking through the little lady who gently said that they could give out food only when everyone was outside. The two men quietly left and took their place in line.

Two men from the church set up a table on the sidewalk where some of the warm clothing was placed. Another man stood outside giving away literature. Evelyn felt very happy to stay inside the van as she placed covers on the big plastic cups filled with hot soup that one of the ladies handed her. She handed these to Delmer who handed the soup out the window to the people who were standing in line. The little lady at the door handed each person a sack lunch. The stack of clothes on the table was gone long before the people were. Finally, each person in line was supplied with a lunch, and the people in the van were on their way again.

The next stop was in front of a dilapidated brick building with broken windows and an old, torn blanket for a door. Children seemed to pour out of the building. Surely they were cold with nothing on their little bare arms and legs, but they looked excited as they grabbed the lunches and began eating right there at the van. One little black-eyed girl stood by the door and watched every move Evelyn made. She smiled, and the little girl smiled back, but when Evelyn tried to talk to the little girl, she ducked her head and ran for the building. Evelyn felt sad. What would happen to this beautiful child?

She had not planned to eat anything, but as the day passed, breakfast seemed to be getting farther and farther away. Everyone else on the van had eaten, and as they continued down the road, Evelyn decided to have a cup of soup. The soup was as delicious as it smelled, and since they were not at their destination, she took a second helping.

Most of the lunches were gone by now, and the second big container of soup was only half full. At the next stop, as the last cup of soup was handed out the window, the person receiving it asked if he could have an empty cup. This was given to him, and he shared one half of his soup with the person next in line. The hardest part of the day was to tell people the food was all gone. Evelyn watched as all hope seemed to fade from the eyes of one large man when he realized there was no more food to share. He bowed his head and slowly walked away.

Evelyn felt sick. *Why had she eaten that soup—and two cups at that?* A car stopped, and a young lady ran to the van exclaiming, "I almost missed you!"

"We are sorry, but we are all out of food."

"Oh, but I want something to read. I don't need food. May I have something to read?" With her hands full of literature, the lady rushed back to the car stopped in the middle of the street and was soon speeding down the road.

Mark started the van, and it was on its way back to the church to leave the empty soup containers, some unused cups, and plastic spoons. They spent a few minutes touring the very old, beautiful church, and then they were heading back to the Van Center with Mark pointing out places of interest along the way.

It was hard for Evelyn to concentrate on what Mark was saying. Those two cups of soup seemed to expand in her stomach, and her head throbbed. She looked over at Delmer. He did not look very well either. She had been so busy either dipping soup or handing it to Delmer, she had not had much chance to observe the people outside the van. He had closer contact with them while handing the soup out the window. She was wondering if he felt absolutely ill from seeing so much poverty too, for she felt she had seen about as much as she could handle.

As the vehicle moved along, Evelyn wondered how she would be able to get more film for her camera. They would soon be leaving for Oregon, and she wanted to get pictures of the Van Center first. Mark mentioned that there was a store about a quarter of a mile away, and she was determined to go there and get some film as soon as possible.

"Delmer, let's go to the store and get some film," Evelyn

pleaded as they climbed the stairs to their room.

"Why didn't you get some before?"

"I couldn't. There was no opportunity."

"Oh, that's okay. You've taken some pictures."

"No, I really want pictures of the Van Center and also of the staff. They will be meeting at eight o'clock in the morning."

By now they had reached their room. Delmer had flopped on the bed and was actually asleep. Evelyn could not believe it! "Delmer," she coaxed, "it will soon be dark. I do not want to go to the store by myself. Please go with me." She hated waking him, but this might be the only chance she would ever have to get pictures of this place with its dedicated staff of workers. She did not plan to miss it.

"You will probably be okay."

"Probably! Are you willing to risk the chance that I might not be?"

"No."

Had he been talking in his sleep? As she talked to him she knew he was not awake. She made plenty of noise getting ready to go, but Delmer continued sleeping. *This has been a hard day for him.* She had no time to lose. It would soon be getting dark. With mixed emotions, she headed out into the cold. Was she being smart? The urge to have pictures of this place drove her on.

Evelyn met Marilyn coming up the stairs, bundled up in a heavy blue jacket with a scarf around her neck. "I am heading for the store to get some film." Evelyn hardly slowed down. "Mark said it is about a quarter of a mile away. But I am not sure which direction to go."

"Isn't Delmer going with you?" Marilyn looked surprised as she spoke.

"No, he's asleep." She answered Marilyn and then rushed down the road in the direction pointed out to her. *I must hurry. It's getting late.* She almost turned back, but "no." She would not let herself do that. Tomorrow would be their last day here, and too many times she had let her fears keep her from doing something she really wanted to do. She hurried along, pushing all the scary things she had heard about New York City out of her mind.

Getting pictures the next day became less and less important as Evelyn realized darkness had already started creeping in. *Why am I doing this? I must be crazy to be out like this in New York, not even knowing where I am going!*

Then she saw someone ahead of her move out of the woods! The person seemed to be in no hurry. All the scary things she had been told about New York City came rushing to her mind. It was too late to turn and run back to the Van Center. Chills ran down her body. She could not see well in the gathering darkness, but knew someone was ahead... leaning against a telephone pole...waiting. Was this person waiting for HER? *Oh, God, You know I NEED You, don't You?*

CHAPTER 13

Evelyn frantically remembered the evening she and Delmer had gone for a walk with Marilyn. On the way home after it had begun to get dark, she had noticed that, if there was a car parked beside the road, Marilyn would lead them out into the street to get around the car. They never walked between the car and the woods. The Van Center was located on a beautiful piece of ground with several acres of trees around it. As Evelyn's heart pounded in her chest, she looked at the person in the gathering darkness and decided to make a big circle out into the street to get around whoever was ahead. She checked for coming cars before stepping off the sidewalk.

"Evelyn!" A voice rang through the cold air. "I thought I would cut through the woods and show you the way to the store. You might not be able to find it."

Evelyn looked at Marilyn. For the first time in her life she knew for sure what angels looked like, but did they always wear heavy blue jackets with scarves around their necks?

Marilyn and Evelyn had a long visit as they slowly walked back home that evening. She shared with Marilyn that she hoped the wonderful feeling of closeness to God would not leave once she got back to the outside world.

"Has Juanita shared with you *Encountering God in Prayer?*" They were heading up the stairs.

"No, but she told me something about it at the airport."

"You know." Marilyn paused in front of the door. "Praying is talking with God as to a friend, and Juanita does not want people to have the idea there is only one way to pray, but this is really special, and I wish you would have a chance to experience it."

"I would love to."

Delmer was still sleeping when Evelyn slipped into the room, wrote him a note, and headed for the car with Marilyn. Marilyn needed to run some errands, and Evelyn was glad to go with her. It was Christmastime, and the decorations were beautiful in this exclusive part of the city, where Marilyn was getting some things that a lady was sending to the Kretschmars.

Later that evening, Marilyn stopped at the room where Delmer and Evelyn were staying. "I hope you do not think I took too much on myself, but since I needed to talk with Juanita anyway, I just mentioned to her how interested you are in *Encountering God in Prayer*. She said she will block off some time for you tomorrow to teach it to you."

What a break! Since Juanita does not push anything on anyone, and Evelyn had not asked, she would have gone home without this special privilege if she and Marilyn had not gotten together that very evening!

Electricity seemed to fill the room Monday morning at worship as the long prayer list was unrolled, answered prayers marked, and new prayer requests added. Each person had a chance to join in the prayer session. This was the time everyone shared experiences of the past week. This was also a time Juanita gathered stories and experiences to share in the newsletter. The reports Delmer received about available air space certainly had not been encouraging. Juanita reminded each one that God gave the Children of Israel land in the Promise Land, and He could also give air space for the TV ministry in New York if that was His will.

The dining room was nearly full when Evelyn stopped the copier long enough to eat lunch. Delmer wanted a copy of the long computer reports on TV air space that were being used in the area—and also of those who had applied for TV frequencies.

At three thirty that afternoon, Juanita left her busy office to keep her appointment with Evelyn.

The Holy Spirit filled the room as Juanita took her step by step through this special *Encountering God in Prayer* experience. God will remove every influence that is not from Him—if we ask God to do this when we kneel to pray. Kneeling by the bed with Juanita, Evelyn asked God to bring to her memory anything that was between her and Him. Then there was a time of waiting. One must give God time to answer. When the answer came, she thanked Him and asked for forgiveness. He then could remove the sin and replace the vacancy with a special gift He had been waiting to give. "God, who do You want me to pray for?" That was another surprise. "Really?" *Maybe there were other people around whom I should be praying for. I must listen and give God more time to speak during my prayers*, she thought.

She spoke to God as a Friend, thanking Him for His many blessings—especially the gift of His Son, Jesus. Again she waited to see if there were any other things God wanted to impress upon her heart before finishing the prayer.

That evening Merlin and Juanita came by the Van Center to take Delmer and Evelyn to Manhattan to see the Macy's store and Christmas decorations. "Dress warmly, and wear good walking shoes." Juanita wanted them to be comfortable.

It was nearly dark when Merlin, Juanita, Delmer, and Evelyn headed for the subway station. There was so much to see. *Thank you, God. Thank you that we are with someone who knows what they are doing and where they are going.*

Evelyn was walking across the street when suddenly Juanita turned, rushed back, grabbed her by the arm, and literally pulled her to the sidewalk as a car sped through a red light.

"You almost were hit!" Juanita was out of breath.

"But the light was green."

"You **still** almost got hit!!"

"I know." Evelyn shuddered as she watched the car cut a corner, go right over the sidewalk, and speed down the street. Green light or no green light, she decided to stay closer to her group and stop losing herself in the beautiful Christmas decorations and huge buildings.

It looked as if each store was trying to outdo the next with its dazzling decorations. A tree, 75 or 80 feet tall, covered with sparkling lights, stood at the Rockefeller Center. Ice skaters glided across the ice beneath the gorgeous "angels" that appeared to be flying above the frozen water. What a fun evening!! Everything had appeared spectacular and striking amid the flashing Christmas lights and decorations. However, by now they were all tired, and it was time to get back to the Van Center.

It was late when Delmer and Evelyn walked through the front door into the lobby of the Center, but Kristy, a young lady who worked there, was still putting the finishing touches on the beautifully decorated Christmas tree. The large tree reached to the top of the high ceiling and spread its branches to hold an assortment of presents. Kristy arranged gifts on the lower limbs of the tree and piled more presents under and around the tree for the guests who would be coming the next evening. Sitting in the kitchen were rows and rows of pies that loving hands had baked that day.

Everyone at the Center seemed excited about the special

joy they would be bringing to their guests, the street people, who had so little. It made little shivers run down Evelyn's back just thinking about the lady who had come the year before and asked, "Is this what heaven will be like?"

For the next three evenings, there would be a different group of people coming to the Center. The buses would pick them up, take them by the warehouse where they would get clean clothes, and bring them to the Christmas celebration. It would be an evening when they could enjoy a delightful program, a gourmet dinner, and gifts.

Along with other things on and surrounding the tree, were gloves, caps, shoes, and lots of toys—especially teddy bears. Each person would have a chance to go to the tree and pick whatever Christmas present he or she wished.

As Delmer and Evelyn climbed the stairs to their room that last night, they knew they would soon be leaving this special place, but it was not the place that was so special. It was God's Spirit working through people for other people, letting them know there is a God who really loves and cares about them.

CHAPTER 14

The eastern light tried to break the darkness that icy morning as the car crawled through the heavy traffic to the John F. Kennedy Airport.

Good-byes had been said, and then someone whispered, "When you get back to those beautiful hills of Oregon, it will seem just like heaven after being in this cement jungle."

Oh, no, Evelyn thought. *This seemed like heaven. How could anyone get closer to heaven on earth than walking in the footsteps of Jesus?*

Later on the plane, Evelyn rested her head on the seat and closed her eyes as the giant aircraft headed its nose toward the western skies. She and Delmer had spent only one short week in New York City, but it had given her the inspiration and courage to forget herself and encourage her husband as he struggled to get new television stations started. She wished she had not said, "Why don't we spend more time working for a television station in New York City, where there is so much support, instead of working so hard for one in Oregon? People are so excited about it here, but at home it seems that no one cares."

What was it God really wanted done in Oregon? Delmer and Evelyn kept praying. Arriving back home in Rogue River, Delmer wrote letters to everyone in New York City he could locate who had an FCC license for television. He also wrote to everyone he could who had applied for one. They spent their time finding addresses, writing letters, and making phone calls. Every day they prayed for wisdom and knowledge to do what needed to be done.

When Evelyn had been visiting with Pastor Michael that day on the van in New York City, he had been talking about prayer and the way God answers prayer—sometimes not the way we would choose at all. She, without thinking, had asked him a very personal question.

"How much time do you spend in prayer each day?"

"At least two and a half hours."

"Two and a half hours!"

"I couldn't cope without it."

She had looked out the window of the van parked on the street corner and saw the people waiting to get their blood pressure taken. Four fellows were there with a big stereo speaker blasting out hard rock music. Jeff had stepped out of the van with some *Signs of the Times* in his hand to speak to the fellows who were obviously there just to be an annoyance to whoever came on the van. Someone mentioned that they might be dealing drugs. It did appear that they had a lot of friends.

When Jeff came back into the van, the music seemed a bit more tolerable. "They aren't bad kids. They probably don't have any other place to go."

"You mean they live right here?" Evelyn looked at the high-rise buildings.

"This is where the people live." Pastor Michael looked out the window. "After living here, you do not take green grass or a front or back yard for granted anymore."

"Wow! I guess you are right," Evelyn said. Pastor Michael should know. He lived right there with his lovely wife and two small children for one reason—to spread the gospel of Jesus Christ. God was giving them the courage, power, and grace to go forward in this difficult place, sharing the love of Jesus with the people who so desperately needed it. Pastor Michael had said the time he spent in prayer just flew by.

Although it seemed there was no possibility of getting a TV frequency, this van project was run on prayer, and they kept praying. They were told there was nothing available.

They were too late. All had been taken—sorry. But Delmer and Evelyn and the Center staff kept praying.

Later, when Merlin and Juanita were in Washington, DC, they asked the specialist in frequencies to run another check on available air space for a TV frequency. He hated to take their money since there definitely was nothing available, but they were sure they wanted another search made. He reluctantly agreed to do so. They prayed for him before they left his office.

When the report came back, there it was—air space right in the Van Center area. Why had no one seen it?

"It is a miracle." The lawyer stared at the papers. "Now that is a word I do not use very often."

It had to be a miracle. There was no question about it.

"God has been saving it for us," the Kretschmars told him.

Because of the problems the FCC had to work out, more than ten years passed before that precious air space in New York City was finally released and awarded to the Greater New York Conference.

CHAPTER 15

Month after month went by as Delmer threw his energy into the project of starting local TV stations in southern Oregon. He had applied for more permits for licenses and anxiously waited to see the outcome.

A public notice must run in the local paper for three days when a license is applied for. When Evelyn's computer printed out the little announcement about the application for a Medford station, she had no idea what the outcome would be from that message. An energetic reporter saw an article in the making and called Delmer. Delmer answered his questions, giving needed information, and again buried himself in his work, too busy to even mention the little incident.

Bill, who read the article in the *Medford Tribune*, called the paper to see how he could get in touch with Delmer. When the telephone rang, Delmer found himself talking to a man who seemed very excited about what he had read in the paper.

"We are having company this evening." Delmer placed the receiver back on the telephone.

Bill arrived around eight o'clock and talked until nearly midnight. He knew of no better way to enter the homes in the community and to spread the good news of Jesus than by starting a television ministry. He shared the fact that most people did not have the vision or knowledge of what a Christian television station could do for the community. He insisted that Delmer be given time to present his project to the attendees at the Gladstone Seventh-day Adventist camp meeting the following week.

"You must let the people know of the possibilities available!" Bill's excitement continued to grow.

It was a great idea, but it appeared to be an impossible one. All the time slots for every meeting were filled and overflowing. With so much potential waiting to be tapped, and no time to speak, Delmer became discouraged.

"I have decided..." He gathered his papers together and put them in a folder. "If the church leaders do not have any interest in local television, I am not going to pursue it any further."

CHAPTER 16

Bill's enthusiasm burned like an unquenchable fire! He had a goal—to see that Delmer could have a few minutes to speak to the people at the Gladstone camp meeting. He insisted the leaders of the church allow Delmer the chance of letting the people know of the opportunity before them. He did not give up with one "no," or two, or three. He did not stop but pressed the issue forward until the goal was realized. Delmer was given two and a half minutes of time on Sabbath morning to tell the audience about the possibility of having Christian television stations.

"There is air space available for television stations," he told the congregation, "but we must act quickly. All air space will soon be taken around the larger cities like Portland and Salem. It is a tremendous opportunity for us to reach every town and every city with the Three Angels Messages while the windows are open."

The announcement was concise and to the point. Evelyn, sitting in the back of the large assembly, felt proud of Delmer for stopping after five minutes. She knew his message touched the hearts of the people.

Many people who were there stopped Delmer to talk about television after the meeting. That Sabbath afternoon, under the trees beside the RV camper, Delmer shared his thoughts with pastors Roger Johnson and Edwin Schwisow along with other visionary people. Bill, also, came and joined the group, talking about the opportunities available.

Arrangements were made for Delmer to speak for ten minutes at the evening meeting in the young adult's pavilion.

Two weeks after camp meeting, Bill and his family moved from Medford to southern California. Delmer continued working ... working ... working with untiring effort.

Edna Mae Anderson, a vivacious, friendly little lady who had worked for the Voice of Prophecy for many years, stopped Delmer one Sabbath morning. "Delmer, I heard your talk about a television station at camp meeting. Why aren't you telling people about it here? I think it is a wonderful idea. I have been telling people, and nobody seems to know anything about it. You need to tell people. I know it can be done."

"Excuse me?"

Edna Mae looked at Delmer and Evelyn in surprise at the look on their faces. "Yes, I mean it. You need to let the people know."

"I thought I was," he answered quietly.

Edna Mae paused a moment. Then she brightened. "I know what we will do. Next Sabbath I am Sabbath School superintendent. I want you and Evelyn to have the mission emphasis. You can tell everyone about the new television project at that time. Everyone needs to hear about this."

Delmer was delighted! He and Evelyn had just returned from the Broadcasters Convention at the Media Center in Thousands Oaks, California. He had talked with Dan Matthews, Danny and Linda Shelton, La Vern Tucker, and many others. Delmer shared his excitement with the congregation that Sabbath morning. After church, people waited to ask him about the new TV station.

This will take a lot of money, Evelyn worried. *I wonder what the pastor thinks. Please, God, guide us and let us know what YOU want done.*

Without telling her husband, she made an appointment with Pastor Steve Poenitz. She shared what Delmer seemed compelled to do. The pastor listened attentively throughout the interview. "Our church has nearly 50 outreach programs," he said. "I can hardly take on any more."

"I am not asking you to help." Evelyn felt confused. "I wouldn't expect that." Her appointment was over, and she stood to leave.

"Evelyn!" Pastor Poenitz stopped her. "Why did you come in for an appointment?"

"Well." She hesitated.

"Was it to see if I approved of this project and to get my blessing?"

"Yes, that is really why I came."

"You certainly have my support. I think it is an outstanding way to reach the community."

That was all she wanted to know. It would be okay with the leadership for them to keep pressing forward. As she walked toward the open door, Pastor Robert Heisler hurried in. Pastor Poenitz turned to Pastor Heisler. "Would you like to spend time working with the Wagners on the television project?"

A big smile spread across Pastor Heisler's face. "Yes. Yes, I surely would!"

CHAPTER 17

Pastor Edwin Schwisow, editor of the *Gleaner*, arranged for meetings to be held in Yakima, Washington, on November 19, 1988. These meetings were meant to inspire the congregation to share the good news of Jesus through broadcasting the love of God to the community and the world. Many people from the Adventist Media Center and those interested in broadcasting were invited to attend. Delmer looked forward to the seminar he would present on the procedures to follow in order to set up a local television station.

"I really want you to come along. I know you have a lot of things to do, but ...," he was talking to Evelyn as he packed his things. "It will be especially enjoyable. The church members are opening up their homes, and we will be staying with the Pierces. I have their address right here."

"Delmer, if I go, couldn't we stay in a motel this time? I am so tired. I would just like to crash."

"No, of course not. All arrangements have been made, and it will cost quite a bit just to drive. We can't afford to stay in a motel when we don't have to."

The fatigue that was trying to become a part of Evelyn's life almost engulfed her as the battle in her heart, which only she knew about, raged. *This isn't fair! I need to rest. I want to stay in a motel!* Her whole being cried out.

However, Jesus won the victory, and peace again settled in what had been the war zone of her mind. She then determined, with God's help, to enjoy every minute of the weekend that lay ahead of her.

Immediately after arriving at the Pierce's house, Evelyn felt at home. These older people had been missionaries for years. Wonderful stories poured from their past. *What an amazing couple,* she thought. It seemed as if she had known them all her life.

Rachael Pierce told Evelyn that Pastor La Vern Tucker, Pastor Jim Brockett with his wife, and also Al McDowell and his wife would be staying with them. Delmer and Evelyn had been the first to arrive, and she continued helping in the kitchen as Mrs. Pierce went to answer the telephone.

Mrs. Pierce seemed a bit troubled when she returned to the kitchen. "I told them at the hospital that I would rather not work tonight." She looked around the room. "However, there is an emergency there, and I am needed. I am sure you can take over with dinner. We will be eating downstairs in the recreation room. There will be a lot of us so we need that space."

She showed Evelyn where the dishes were kept, and then she was gone. Dr. Warren D. Pierce and Delmer set up the long table downstairs, and the other guests began arriving. Of course, in the mission field, whoever happened to be available filled in and did what needed to be done, and these people were true missionaries.

Beginning the descent of the long flight of stairs with a large bowl of boiling hot vegetables in her hands, Evelyn felt her heel catch on something. Trying to release her foot, she lost her balance—holding tightly to the bulky bowl with both hands, she began to fall down the long steep stairway!!

God, help me! her heart cried out. She could almost feel the boiling contents of the hefty dish burning her flesh.

At that moment, Evelyn felt a steadying grip on her right

shoulder, and her balance was completely restored as she made her way down the stairs to the last step and set the steaming food on the long table. *Thank you, God. Thank you for saving me from disaster,* she silently prayed with bowed head, marveling at the answer to her prayer. Her body shook at the thought of what had just happened. **She had felt the hand of her guardian angel!**

She then put the last touches on dinner and called everyone to come eat. The meal turned into more fun than a picnic with everyone sharing experiences and getting acquainted.

After eating, Al McDowell and Delmer went for a long walk. Al had so much to share with Delmer now that the radio station in Boise, Idaho, had become a reality. He had worked so hard to get it started, and now it was a success. It had been more than a year since their last walk together at Thousand Oaks, California, during the Broadcasters Convention. The walk Al's wife and Evelyn took turned out to be quite a bit shorter, but then the fellows had not stopped to wash the dishes either. *And to think I had wanted to stay in a motel!*

Breakfast the next morning seemed even more enjoyable than the meal the night before. Everyone appeared to be rested after a good night's sleep. Evelyn sat spellbound listening to Pastor La Vern Tucker tell of experiences in the Philippines—stories that would never be told in *The Quiet Hour Echoes.*

Pastor Tucker spoke for church. During the afternoon meeting, he said, "I have a man here on the platform with me who lives television. He eats it, talks it, and sleeps it. If he talked in his sleep, I am sure it would be about television." He smiled at Delmer.

That evening Delmer presented his seminar. As Evelyn

waited for him to finish, she visited with Pastor Tucker who needed to catch an early morning flight back to California.

"You don't need to wait here at the church," she told Pastor Tucker, as she opened her purse. "Get a key for the Pierces' house and drive our car there. We'll come with the Pierces."

While Pastor Tucker got a key from Dr. Pierce, she reached into her purse for her set of keys. *Where are they? I know they were here.* Again she went through every compartment in her purse—and there were many. Pastor Tucker continued waiting as Evelyn looked through her purse again, and again.

"They are here. I know they are here!"

"Don't worry about it." Pastor Tucker tried to make her feel better. "There is a place here at the back of the church where I can get a little rest."

Where, oh where could those keys be? She looked in her purse again. There they were! The big ring of keys was right where it was supposed to be all the time!!

Evelyn grabbed her keys and quickly went to find Pastor Tucker. As she searched the corridor, she found him busily talking with some people who seemed to be in a desperate need to talk with him. She did not interrupt. After Delmer's seminar finished, everyone waited for Pastor Tucker until his conversation came to an end. The people thanked Pastor Tucker profusely for his help. *Hmm. Did an angel hide my keys so Pastor Tucker could minister to those people?* Evelyn felt a wave of awe.

What a day!! What a God!! God's presence had seemed to fill the place. *Thank you. Thank you, God.* Delmer slowly drove the car through the darkness back to the Pierce's home. *And to think that I wanted to stay in a motel!*

CHAPTER 18

When Pastor Heisler threw his heart, soul, and energy, along with his talents, into the television project, it sprouted wings and began to fly.

Better Life Television (BLTV), a nonprofit corporation, became a reality. It just needed to get the transmitters up and start broadcasting. Board members were chosen from each Seventh-day Adventist church in the Rogue Valley. Pastor Heisler became the new president. Many others also gave time and talents to the soon-to-be broadcasting television station.

The Adventist Broadcasters Association Convention was again held at the Media Center in Thousand Oaks, California.

"How are you going to get an audience?" a man sitting across the breakfast table at the convention asked Delmer. That was a question he had not spent much time thinking about. Before that meal finished, he felt convinced that there needed to be a TV studio in Grants Pass where local programs could be produced and aired. The community needed to see local programs. The cable companies would be more responsive to air the programs if part of them were local.

Much time was spent in prayer asking God how they should move forward. A program committee was formed to outline the community's needs. What would be the best way for Better Life Television to share God's love to the Rogue Valley? People from all of the southern Oregon Seventh-day Adventist churches needed to be involved.

The principal of Grants Pass Junior Academy made arrangements so Better Life Television could have one of the rooms to finish and use for a studio in the new building being built for the academy. This room could be used by BLTV until the school needed the space and BLTV could get another place of its own.

Without a telephone or even a television set, BLTV set up their new studio in a room at the end of a long hall in the new school building. A satellite dish sat on the roof above the studio.

Louise Teague, a retired Bible worker, lived close to the school. Her phone became the official telephone for the studio. Her TV was used to view the programs and pick up the feed from the station going up to Mt. Baldy. From there the transmitter sent it out over the valley. She left her house at nine o'clock in the morning to turn on the station, and then go home to see if it came on her TV. If it did not, she would go back to the school to see what happened. Mornings weren't so bad, but on some nights after dark, she had some scary experiences as she returned to the school to turn off the station. The staff, especially Louise, rejoiced when Better Life Television was able to transmit programs 24 hours a day.

Charles Betz, a retired minister, and his lovely wife Harriet, were Delmer and Evelyn's neighbors and close friends. Pastor Betz developed the mission statement with help from other members of the board. Although the couple was very busy—Pastor Betz wrote Sabbath School programs for the Primary Department in the Far East; Harriet put this information into the computer; they presented Sabbath School seminars throughout the Far East, England, and North America; and wrote articles and books—he and Harriet were never too busy for Delmer and Evelyn or Better

Life Television.

Thank you, God, for the visionary people who are willing to step forward and support this television ministry.

God picked people with various experiences fitted for the challenges confronting the new struggling mission outreach. He opened doors and broke down walls that might easily have aborted the project.

Among those supporting the project were Oliver and Fredonia Jacques. Their background included pastoral evangelism, mission service, administration posts in a university, hospitals, and the House of Representatives. In these positions, Oliver had dealt with many world-renown people, including five US presidents.

A firm advocate of "volunteerism," Oliver held leading positions in many community and national organizations. His experience was a godsend in promoting and developing Better Life Television.

Fredonia, an artist, musician, author, and mother of four, was recognized as a founder of the profession of hospital patient representatives. Her books on the subject are used in hospitals throughout the nation and overseas. Before leaving Grants Pass, she wrote a book on the childhood experiences of Ellen White, who was Oliver's great grandmother. This book, with pictures she painted, became a part of a series of children's programs produced by Better Life Television.

The Jacques were a marvelous help to the new television station. It seemed to be in God's timing that they were in Grants Pass for several years.

CHAPTER 19

Each station cost thousands of dollars, and people sacrificed as God impressed their hearts. The station in Rogue River was a small one. It would cost only twelve thousand dollars. Only? Where would twelve thousand dollars come from? The congregation was struggling to pay for their new church building.

Asking for money—oh, how Evelyn hated it. Not that she asked for any. No way. But she still felt she was in the middle of it. Fortunately, God was in control.

The James E. Miller Peace Memorial, (JEMM) was a nonprofit corporation that was being dissolved in another state. Dave and Ann Miller Reed wanted the funds to be transferred to Better Life Television.

Letters went back and forth to the Secretary of State in Minnesota with questions and answers. Should the money leave the state? Is that what the founder of the corporation, Ann's father, would want? Finally the JEMM board members decided that Better Life Television would receive eight thousand dollars.

The eight thousand dollars would go to help pay for the new transmitter to be located on Tin Pan Peak behind the Rogue River Seventh-day Adventist Church.

The next Sabbath Delmer took twenty minutes telling the congregation at the Rogue River Church about Better Life Television. If they could raise four thousand dollars, there would be a television station for the people in Rogue River.

He had already climbed the four thousand feet up Tin Pan Peak and had found a good site for the transmitter. The construction permit was in his hands. He had received permission from the Bureau of Land Management to put the equipment up there and transmit to the area.

The church in Rogue River accepted the challenge to raise four thousand dollars—knowing that the other eight thousand dollars would be taken care of.

Praise God! Miracles were happening, and then— Monday came. Evelyn, on her way to town, picked up the mail. In her hand lay a letter from the Secretary of State of Minnesota. She ripped open the long envelope. *Could it be the money needed to order the equipment for the station?* No check. Only a letter. The letter should have been edged in black. "I must tell you that it has been voted that none of the money from the corporation will be going out of the state..." Evelyn laid the letter down.

How could this be happening? Why? Oh, why, God? If we were going to get this letter, why couldn't it have come before Delmer gave that talk at the Rogue River Church?

Evelyn drove down the road, tears blinding her eyes. Then thoughts began jumping into her mind—thoughts foreign to her thinking—thoughts so strong that she pulled the car to the side of the road and began writing. She continued writing as new ideas crowded in.

After Evelyn arrived home from town that evening, she went to the computer and composed a letter to the Secretary of State from the daughter of the deceased parents, Hanes and Margarette Miller. Delmer and Evelyn took the letter to Ann.

"Could you claim this letter?" She handed the letter to Ann. Ann read the letter. She looked amazed.

"Yes, I certainly can. That is exactly the way I feel. I'll be glad to sign and send the letter right away."

Time hung heavy as prayers ascended to God day after day and week after week. Would another miracle happen? Finally, the long-awaited letter came from the Secretary of State of Minnesota. Evelyn trembled as she s-l-o-w-l-y pulled the letter out of the envelope.

CHAPTER 20

Evelyn sat in the car beside the mailbox. In her hand lay a letter from the Secretary of State of Minnesota. It felt as valuable as if it had been written in gold. "After reconsideration..." She read the words again. "It has been decided that we can send the money out of state. Better Life Television will receive eight thousand dollars."

Numerous people had been praying for this outcome. However, many of the people at the Rogue River Church never knew the trauma going on behind the scenes. But, by November 1990, they did know the trauma of trying to bury 4,000 feet of wire straight up Tin Pan Peak.

Volunteers came to help with the slow and dangerous work. The dune buggy, with power drive on all six wheels, could climb part of the way up the mountain— with a couple of guys sitting on the hood to hold it down. Then the brakes went out, and the driver, along with the two guys sitting on the hood of the dune buggy, felt they would rather get their thrills another way!

Evelyn called around, hoping to find some mules or something to help haul things up the steep mountainside, but manpower seemed the best option. Manpower or boy power—the Pathfinders were terrific. What energy! They loved the excitement.

A friend of Better Life Television who was a hot air balloon operator graciously volunteered to lift the precious television equipment to the top of the mountain. On the appointed day, Delmer and Evelyn were at the church before daybreak. She had brought lots of food for anyone needing it. It would be a long day.

Soon the volunteers began arriving in trucks and cars. Men started hiking up the 4,000-foot mountain and lined up along the side of it to hold the 50 to 70-foot ropes as the equipment was raised into the air. Hopefully the men holding the ropes could guide the hot air balloon to the right spot on top of Tin Pan Peak.

The man arrived with the huge hot air balloon. He laid out the massive 70-foot "envelope." Then he started the fire to raise the balloon while people stood around taking pictures.

Oh, no! Evelyn thought. The wind started blowing— blowing the wrong way! Delmer needed more walkie-talkie radios to communicate with the men. Evelyn jumped into the truck and headed out to get some.

Going down Main Street in Rogue River, she noticed people walking along looking up at the sky. Others were pulling over in cars. Then she saw the hot air balloon heading in the direction of Grants Pass. The massive box of BLTV equipment kept swinging back and forth held by long ropes hanging from the balloon. Where was it going? How could they stop it?

By the time she got back to the church, the equipment had settled down onto a parking lot in town, and men with trucks were retrieving it. After his balloon had been taken off course by the wind, the operator offered to pay part of the fee for a helicopter to take the equipment to the top of the mountain. The equipment would get another air ride!

After an hour or so, the sound of a helicopter skimming through the air was like music to the waiting volunteers at the Rogue River Church parking lot.

A couple of men who were needed to help assemble the equipment, but were unable to climb the mountain, joined the pilot inside the helicopter. The equipment was heavy! Could the helicopter lift it? Every ounce of weight had to be carefully calculated. Volunteers seemed to hold their breath as the motor roared. Slowly, ever so slowly, the big box of equipment, tied to the helicopter, began to move as the helicopter struggled to lift the weight into the air.

Every eye was watching as it went higher and higher! The volunteers prayed and watched it make a circle and settle down on top of the mountain. So many hopes and dreams and prayers accompanied that precious cargo! There would be a second trip for the helicopter when the high-powered transmitter needed to go up.

Just before darkness covered the trail, Delmer, Pastor Bob Heisler, and the other volunteers who stayed on top of the mountain to assemble and finish putting the equipment in place came back down the steep mountainside. Part of the time they walked. Part of the time they slid. Sometimes they fell, but they all made it back safely. And on July 9, 1991, Channel 67 was airing Better Life Television's programs from Tin Pan Peak.

CHAPTER 21

By the year 1993, Ann Reed, studio manager, made everything flourish. Soon local programs were being aired with the help of Dave Reed, head cameraman, and his many assistants.

Better Life Television needed more room. They had outgrown the one classroom being used at the school for the past few years.

When construction time arrived, the mayor of Grants Pass helped move the first shovel of dirt for the foundation. Volunteers made this project a possibility. One volunteer, Orland Davis, nearly 90 years old, climbed the tall ladders to the 20-foot ceiling. It did not seem to be a challenge as he continued working on all of the electrical wiring for the whole building.

Robert Mitchell, Evelyn's brother, had a dream of getting Better Life Television started in his home town of Klamath Falls. He worked with the pastor, and a church business meeting was scheduled. Delmer was invited to go to Klamath Falls to present the possibilities of the Klamath Falls Seventh-day Adventist Church having their own Christian television station.

The chairs in the room were nearly filled by the time Delmer and Evelyn arrived. Delmer gave his presentation and then the people began asking questions.

The telephone rang, and the pastor had to leave. One of the members of his congregation, a well-known citizen in the community, had been rushed to the hospital.

Evelyn felt that many of the people who stayed after the meeting were afraid to even think of raising so much money. The pastor's wife talked with Delmer. "This is for your gas." She slipped a check into his hand. "Thank you for coming. This church cannot afford the station now, but we do appreciate your coming over."

Wow! They appreciated our coming! Of all of the places we have gone, this is the only time anyone has offered to pay for our gas, Evelyn thought.

Money started coming to the Klamath Falls Seventh-day Adventist Church marked "For the new television station." The first check was a big one and a total surprise. More checks kept coming saying the same thing—"For the new television station." Someone had written a notice in the Klamath Falls newspaper that those who wished to give a memorial gift in honor of a well-known, beloved man who had just died should send their check to the Klamath Falls Seventh-day Adventist Church for the new television station.

Trinity Broadcasting put their station up for sale, asking about a third of the going price. Robert put his little portable television in the car and drove all around the area to see how far the signal reached. The signal was reaching out very well. By now people were convinced that God wanted Better Life Television to send the news of Christ's soon coming to the people living in the Klamath Falls area. Committees were formed, and sacrifices were made. Better Life Television became a reality in another southern Oregon town.

"It wasn't nearly as hard as I had expected." The pastor's wife smiled as she and Evelyn were visiting later.

All over southern Oregon people sacrificed money and hours and hours of time. It felt like a wonderful, close family working together with so many dedicated people.

Because of the many mountains around the area, the TV signal was not available everywhere. It followed the line of sight, although it did curve over or around the mountaintops to some extent. The signal could not get through a lot of trees or insulation into a house very well.

For this reason, the antennas were usually set up on the roofs of the houses, but not always. The installers would take the little portable TV that was tuned to BLTV and walk around to see where the signal came in the best. Sometimes the signal was so weak that they needed to put on a booster device so the program would be nice and clear. This was expensive, but BLTV bought boosters in quantities and got a discount. People were sold the equipment at cost, but the installers never charged for their hours of time, gallons of gas, or the wear and tear on their vehicles.

All volunteers gave tirelessly of their time and talents, never expecting anything in return—only the ultimate return—seeing people in the kingdom because of their love and labor.

CHAPTER 22

Huge fire-fighting bombers roared overhead! Helicopters dropped to the river and scooped up big buckets of water! They made their way to the hungry flames that were devouring everything in their pathway a hot August day in 1993. Brave men driving the caterpillars and other fire-fighting equipment worked endlessly trying to contain the terrible destruction!

The Seventh-day Adventist church was located at the bottom of the mountain. People working in the church were sent away by the firemen. Television Channel 67 sat at the top of the mountain. It had been an extremely hot, dry summer, and the fire fighters had been working overtime in many parts of southern Oregon. People could only wait and pray as they watched the fire reach the top of the mountain.

Better Life Television Channel 67 went dead. Evelyn answered the telephone. "From our place, it looks like the tower is surrounded by fire. The fire has reached the top of the mountain!" Ann's words came in strong and clear above the wild beating of Evelyn's heart.

"Oh, no!" She felt her body grow weak. Hundreds of people were praying. Would God decide to spare the church? What about Channel 67? Psalm 91 seemed very precious, and she read it over and over. Sometimes God does not choose to save His property from destruction. Would He do it this time?

Oh, dear God, no matter what happens, please some way,

somehow make this bring glory to Your name. After that prayer, she felt a peace that controlled her racing heart as she claimed promises and prayed for God's will to be done.

The planes kept dropping large loads of fire retardant. Helicopters kept unloading their tubs of water. Men on the ground worked through the night. Finally, the raging fire became only smoldering embers. As soon as the firemen gave their approval, Dave Reed and Delmer climbed the mountain. They noticed that the electrical cable had been cut by some equipment while the brave firefighters had fought the fire. All around the tower brush that had been cleared and thrown into piles was now ashes. The tower stood straight and tall surrounded by the destruction that had stopped within five or ten feet all around. Had heavenly angels been present holding back the flames?

In two years, three fires threatened to destroy God's property on and near Tin Pan Peak. One of the fires had been started by someone in the tall, dry grass close to the church. A wind whipped the flames straight toward the building. The firefighters rushed in but would not have been able to save the church. Before the fire reached the church, the wind made a 180-degree change. The firemen were able to contain the flames on that side of the then fast-moving fire! The firefighters believed that a Power greater than theirs had saved the church. Dave and Ann were there. "We have a prayer chain." Ann was talking to the tired, amazed firefighters. "We have been praying that God would save His property."

Again God's name was glorified.

CHAPTER 23

"Evelyn. Please come help me!"

Evelyn heard the call coming from the bedroom. She quickly dropped what she was doing and dashed in the direction of the voice.

Standing in the doorway, she gasped. There stood Delmer all tied up in ropes and a strange looking harness.

"What is that, and whatever are you doing?"

"I need help." Delmer looked frustrated. "Please try to figure out the directions so we can get this right."

"What is it?"

"It is a climbing harness."

"You bought a climbing harness!! What in the world for?"

Other people had climbed the towers. Pastor Bob's son had rock climbing equipment and knew how to climb. Pastor Bob was also a climber. Delmer had never climbed in his life, and here he stood hooked up in this paraphernalia.

"I have to climb the tower and then go out on the side to fix the equipment. You don't want me to fall do you?"

"No. Of course not!"

"Then we need to know how to do this right. If it isn't right, it might come loose while I'm up there." He adjusted some more straps.

"Oh, Delmer, can't you get someone else to do it? You've never climbed before!"

"I've climbed these towers several times. It will just be safer with this equipment."

"Oh."

The towers stretched up to 100 feet in the air where the antenna sat. If water made its way into the connectors, the reception became poor. Then someone had to climb the tower and dry or replace the parts.

One morning the wind moaned around the house, and the rain poured down sideways, pounding the wet grass. The news commentator made things worse by saying the snow level would be dropping.

"I just talked to Pastor Bob." Delmer was gathering his things together. "We must go to the mountain today and work on the tower. If the snow gets too deep we'll never make it." Then he was gone.

Snow was probably already covering the narrow little road that clung to the side of the mountain. Darkness fell, and still, water poured off the eaves of the house. Quoting Psalm 91 always made Evelyn feel better. An hour passed. Then another hour crawled by.

She watched as the long hand of the clock went around its face again. She tried to remember that God could take care of Delmer and Pastor Bob on the mountain as well as anywhere else. The short hand on the clock had migrated past ten o'clock and had nearly reached eleven o'clock when the telephone shattered the stillness of the night.

"I am calling to let you know Bob and Delmer are okay." Anita Heisler's sweet voice sounded relieved and happy. "On the way down the mountain, something happened to Delmer's car. They just got here but didn't stop to eat or anything. Bob is bringing Delmer straight home."

"I'll have something hot ready for them when they get here." She hurried to the kitchen. "Thank you for calling!"

When Pastor Bob and Delmer walked in, Evelyn saw that

they were dripping wet. However, they insisted they were just fine while they emptied the plates set before them.

"I hit a rock that took out the oil pan on my car. It will have to be towed in for repairs." Delmer looked tired and was soon sound asleep after Pastor Bob hurried home so he, too, could get a little rest.

During the early morning hours, Evelyn listened to her husband's deep, regular breathing. He was safe and sleeping in a warm bed. *He surely keeps my prayer life active. Oh, how I wish he wouldn't take so many chances!*

One evening Delmer came home exhausted and flopped onto a chair. "I'm glad I took your dad's Bronco today."

"Why?"

"Well, I was going up this little road and had to go through a gate. That was no problem, but when I came back, the gate had been padlocked shut. I had to make my own road down the mountain to get home."

"Oh, Delmer." She shuddered. "You surely keep your guardian angels busy. You would have worried me if you had stayed up there all night. I never would have known where to even start looking for you."

"Really? I try to be careful."

"I know you don't want to spend the money, but...," Evelyn spoke slowly. She had thought this over carefully, and this was one time she did not plan to take "no" for an answer. "We are going to get a cellular telephone that you can take with you whenever you go to the mountaintops."

CHAPTER 24

It had been another hot, dry summer. Delmer had spent a lot of time on the mountains.

Why did the transmitters have to go down when the weather was so uncomfortable? Evelyn wondered. In the winter, the snow or falling ice would damage the antennas. Sometimes the connectors would get moisture in them. Now it was summertime, and the heat was affecting the components in the transmitters. They put out heat themselves, and with the atmospheric temperature around 106 degrees, they could not stand the heat and the whole thing failed.

Evelyn had been hoping that Delmer would take off work for a few days, so they could go visit Judy, their daughter, her husband, Michael, and their grandchildren. Now she had given up hope of Delmer going at all. She would have to go by herself if she was going to go visit the kids. Too much was going on at Better Life Television. *What a bummer,* she thought. *Will we always be this busy?*

She packed her suitcase and got the car checked. The tires were okay, and she filled the gas tank. If she left home by three thirty the next morning, she should be at her daughter's place before the worst heat of the day.

Why is Delmer always so busy? Evelyn hated driving long distances alone. What she didn't know was that God was about to perform some miracles for her. The time passed quickly and the temperature climbed. It was 109 degrees by the time she went through Williams, California, on her way to Middletown.

Judy lived in a gated community called Hidden Valley. Evelyn stopped at the gate, and Judy was called before the gate could be opened for her. Her car barely made it through the gate and stopped three houses down the road from Judy's home. Judy walked down the road, and the neighbors came, but no one was able to get the car started. It was pushed into the neighbor's driveway. Michael checked the car when he came home from work. He just shook his head. "I don't know how you even made it here.

Your fuel filter is completely plugged with dirt!"

Thank you, God, for getting me here safely.

By the time Evelyn had walked the short distance to Judy's home, she had a throbbing headache. It must have been heat exhaustion, for it took her three or four days to begin to feel like herself again. *What would have happened if the car had stopped while I was on my way?* She knew it was God who had gotten her safely to her destination.

Too soon it was time to head for home. Michael told her not to worry about the car. "It is all fixed. I got a new fuel filter. You will be fine now. It was a miracle you even made it down here!"

Evelyn left very early in the morning. Her heart was singing. God was taking care of her. The heat had abated a bit. Hour after hour she drove up I-5. She stopped and ate the lunch Judy had made, filled her gas tank, and was on her way again. The Christian radio station was telling of the blessing of knowing God. If only the young people could figure it out—that giving their hearts to Jesus and following Him was the most wonderful, electrifying life they could possibly live. She knew what they were saying was the truth.

God had protected her on the way down to her daughter's place. She could have died from the heat. God was her closest Friend, and she felt His presence. Evelyn was deep in concentration—**too deep.**

Another car was also speeding up I-5. The speed limit was 70 miles an hour. That was probably the speed Evelyn was traveling. The car ahead of her was going slower, so she checked her side mirror—at least she thought she did—and started to pull into the left lane.

As she glanced out the side window, she saw the top of a little fast-moving black sports car passing. Automatically she turned her car to the right, but it turned more than she had expected—much more.

The cement wall to her right appeared to be moving fast—straight at her!!! She turned to miss the wall and the turn sent her shooting straight toward the other two cars! All of this happened in just seconds. She was only a few feet from the two other vehicles, and her car was **out of control!! Evelyn's guardian angel took control at that instant.**

It happened so fast there was no realization of time. Her car was just going down the road following the car she had started to pass in the first place.

It was unbelievable! She was alive and unhurt! *Oh, Thank you! Thank you, God!* She actually glanced to her right, but she did not see her guardian angel. She felt the presence and knew she was not alone.

Evelyn noticed the little black sports car following her at some distance behind. It took them miles before they got the courage to pass again. The driver of the sports car had to have seen what happened. She wondered, *Are they praising and thanking God too?*

CHAPTER 25

A broadcast permit was applied for on Mt. Bluie, which is one of the higher mountains in the area. Delmer and Pastor Bob worked hard to install the transmitter and antenna on the mountain. Numerous trips had to be made to the transmitter site, as there was a problem with matching the antenna to the transmitter.

The antenna was almost 100 feet from the ground, which is 4,000 feet above the valley floor. The antenna was four feet out from the tower, attached by a metal brace. The coaxial connector on the antenna had to be replaced, as it was faulty. That meant Pastor Bob had to crawl four feet out on the metal brace to remove the connector and install a new one.

It was a cold December day. The wind was blowing. The sky was covered with clouds about 100 feet above the tower. The clouds were moving at a fast pace as the storm winds blew them on their way. The wind was blowing through the tower and the guy-wires made a howling sound. It felt, to Pastor Bob, as if the tower was swaying back and forth about 15 feet in a slow twisting motion as he climbed up the cross bracing of the tower.

Is this a good day to be doing this? Pastor Bob wondered as he climbed. Upon reaching the 100-foot level, he rested for a moment before venturing out on the four-foot brace to remove the connector. With a sea of angry clouds above and swaying back and forth on the tower 100 feet from the ground, he was hesitant to venture out on the antenna brace.

The angry clouds above and the 4,000-foot view of the Rogue Valley below was not an attractive sight.

Pastor Bob paused for a moment to pray. *Lord, I know You calmed the sea of Galilee one night, and You do have power over the wind and the waves. It's scary up here. I'm not asking You to do it, but it sure would be nice if You would make the wind quit blowing while I am out on that brace. This is a mission for Your kingdom, and I want Your will to be done. Amen.*

Pastor Bob methodically checked his safety harness and then slowly made his way out onto the metal brace. It took about half an hour to peel away the protective plastic tape from the connector, remove and replace the connector, and then re-tape it to make it waterproof.

As he turned from the antenna and reached for the tower, the thought came to his mind. *I have been out here on this metal brace for half an hour, and I haven't noticed the tower swaying once. Could it be that I was concentrating so much on the connector that I did not notice the tower swaying in the wind, or did God actually stop the wind while I was working? Who cares,* he thought, *my prayer was answered.*

CHAPTER 26

On a cold, foggy morning in October 1998, Evelyn sat at her computer. She still felt awed just thinking of the way the Lord had saved her life coming home from Judy's when her car went out of control. *We serve a God of miracles*, she thought. *I need to write an article.* Evelyn knew God didn't always save individuals from accidents. *Bad things happen to good people. We need to trust Him. That is what He asks.*

The telephone rang. She picked up the receiver and heard a voice. "Is this Mrs. Wagner? You need to get to the hospital as quickly as possible. There has been a bad accident, and you need to get here as soon as you can if you want to see Robert Mitchell before he goes into surgery. It doesn't look good."

She could hardly think. "My mother was also with Bob. How is she?"

"It was a multi-car accident. I do not know where all the people were taken."

"Oh, Aunt Beryl!" Evelyn called her aunt before rushing out the door. "Mother and Bob were on their way to Medford. There has been a terrible accident."

"Where is Delmer?" She could hear her aunt catch her breath.

"I don't know. He is on the mountain somewhere fixing something for Better Life Television."

"Shall I go with you? I'll be ready when you get here."

They saw the police cars stopped where the accident happened as they rushed to the hospital. Mercifully they did not see the little white car her brother had been driving.

When they arrived at the hospital, Bob was already in surgery. "I will go see where your mother was taken." Aunt Beryl left, and Evelyn collapsed in a chair.

"I suppose you know your mother was killed in the accident." A sad-faced nurse was standing in front of Evelyn. The waiting room began to spin. *Oh, God, no!*

Aunt Beryl made some telephone calls. Soon Delmer and Evelyn's son, Ed, and wife, Linda, were by her side. Ed took over handling whatever needed to be done. He was able to contact Delmer, and other friends also came to the hospital. Bob gradually improved and began to heal. There were hard days ahead, with many prayers ascending to heaven on his behalf. God heard, and Bob's health slowly returned.

Evelyn's parents had enjoyed Better Life Television more than anyone else she knew. At one time Delmer said, "It would be worth all the work I put into Better Life Television just to see how much your parents enjoy it."

After her daddy died, it was hard to keep her mother from giving all she had to Better Life Television when the station desperately needed money.

"Mother," she advised, "make out a will and give what you want at that time. You may need this money."

Now, with Better Life Television expanding and, as always, needing money, the inheritance from Evelyn's parents helped it move forward. Soon Jesus will come, and they will be pleased with what their money was able to accomplish.

CHAPTER 27

"What's going on?" Delmer asked himself, as he scanned the documents before him. He had just come from the mailbox with the usual pile of junk mail along with a letter or two that appeared important. Delmer had opened a letter from Christian Life Broadcasting, a television station located in Utah, sending him a bunch of forms from the FCC. After a long telephone call and checking the information on the FCC website, Delmer realized Better Life Television had just lost over half of their stations!

"Our stations are gone!" he exclaimed as he picked up some documents and brought them to Evelyn so she could study them. "They now belong to Christian Life Broadcasting!"

No one knew how this could possibly have happened. It usually takes months of red tape to change one station to another owner. Now as far as the FCC was concerned Christian Life Broadcasting owned most of Better Life Television's stations.

Delmer and Evelyn were devastated. All of their energy had gone into trying to raise money for a new full-power station, Channel 30. Now over half of the channels Better Life Television owned had been taken away from them!

Evelyn prayed while Delmer and the owner of Christian Life Broadcasting worked together with the FCC doing what could be done with the stations that, over the last decade, Delmer had been working so hard to start.

They did not tell many people about this crisis. Losing the

stations seemed too shocking to even talk about! He worked to straighten out the problem while she continually pleaded with God for another miracle. When Delmer asked the church to please put BLTV on the prayer list, there was a big reason—a reason no one could have ever dreamed of happening.

So many people felt it was presumptuous for Better Life Television to even be thinking about trying to get a full-power television station. My, would the supporters be horrified if they knew Better Life Television no longer owned half of the stations it already had acquired!

It took months for the FCC to finally realize that they were the one who had made the mistake. How could this have happened? The FCC doesn't tolerate mistakes! What a relief when those stations were back in Better Life Television's name!! Delmer did not know then that if those stations had not been put back into Better Life Television's name, **in time**, it would never have gotten the license for Channel 30, but that is another story.

Meanwhile back in New York City, things were beginning to happen for the television station that Delmer and so many others had worked to secure many years before.

The Kretschmars had retired and moved to Florida. The FCC had finally released the construction permit to the SDA Community Services in 1998, giving them 18 months to have the television station running. Those eighteen months passed without anyone accomplishing the job of getting the station on the air. In 1999, Amazing Facts evangelist Kim Kjaer was in New York City conducting meetings. He learned about the license for a station and that it was about to expire. He filed for an extension with the FCC the very day of the deadline. The FCC granted this final extension, giving the license another 18 months of life which would expire on April 10, 2001.

On September 18, 2000, Pastor Bill Bremmer was elected to serve as the Community Services Director of the Van Ministry in New York City. In November 2000, he shared with Greater New York Conference President Dionisio Olivo some of his dreams for the Van Ministry, including moving forward with Channel 29—the long-awaited TV station. He was encouraged to explore the possibility. Others were not as encouraging. They called the idea of a TV station in New York City "a pipe dream."

"It's not a pipe dream. With God, it is possible..." Pastor Bremmer was determined to do his best to make this station come to life, but until March there were no financial backers for the station. There had been too many years when nothing had happened in relation to it. But God blessed, and the SDA Community Services was able to use the funds that had been saved up for the project. The Community Services Board made a bold move and voted to go forward. The transmitter and the antenna were ordered.

On March 8, the company from which they were purchasing the antenna and the transmitter confirmed that they would have the transmitter and antenna shipped "by the end of the month"—March 31. That would give them ten days to set up the antenna and the transmitter to meet the deadline. If they were not broadcasting by midnight on April 10, the permission to construct TV Channel 29 would be invalid, and the station that was granted years ago would probably be given to someone else. In the words of the lawyer, "It would evaporate."

During the last week of March, the transmitter was completed, but it now became apparent that the antenna would not be. It was April 3. Seven days before the deadline to broadcast or lose everything. They didn't have the antenna, but in a major leap of faith, they went ahead and paid for the transmitter. Because of the late date, it was decided to rent a truck in Pennsylvania and bring the transmitter to the site. The transmitter was set up, but they were still unable to turn it on without an antenna.

Pastor Bremmer tried to obtain information from the manufacturer of the antenna company, but to no avail. The company was in Oregon and would not release any information on when they expected to have the antenna completed. When he mentioned the urgency of the project to the consumer relations representative who worked at the manufacturing site, she told him they would not commit to any specific day to send the antenna and that he was wrong for calling them directly. She said he should deal only with their agent, the company he was buying the antenna from.

It was now Wednesday, April 4. Pastor Bremmer called the company he was buying the antenna from. The salesman informed him that their company would not promise the antenna until April 12!

Chapter 28

Pastor Bremmer called Juanita Kretschmar in Florida to pray about the desperate situation. She told him there was one man who had the tenacity to see to it that the antenna would get to New York: Delmer Wagner.

Pastor Bremmer called Delmer and discovered that he "happened" to be a representative of that same antenna company and had bought several antennas from them himself. Pastor Bremmer told Delmer the situation and named the customer representative that he had tried to deal with. Delmer glanced at his watch. It was 4:53 p.m., Pacific Standard Time.

"I have only five minutes to call her before she gets off work." Quickly, Delmer dialed the company, which was located in Medford.

The next morning, Thursday, Pastor Bremmer received a call from the manufacturing company telling him the antenna was ready to be shipped. The only way the antenna could be shipped was via a DC-8 aircraft in Portland, Oregon—if they had someone to drive it from their plant in Medford to Portland five hours away. Delmer told Pastor Bremmer he knew of a man who might be willing to put the antenna on the back of his pickup truck and drive it straight to the airport in Portland.

To Pastor Bremmer, the idea of a 21-foot, 178-pound antenna strapped on the back of a 14-foot pickup truck was not a comforting thought. An accident of the antenna falling and breaking the SDA Community Services 14-year quest for an Adventist TV station in Greater New York was unthinkable.

But he accepted Delmer's offer to find someone to take the antenna to Portland.

Marvin and Shirley Dirksen accepted the challenge and rushed to get ready to leave for the airport in Portland. The huge piece of equipment was strapped to the top of the vehicle they would be driving to Portland. Evelyn spent the day in prayer for Marvin and Shirley's protection as she went about her duties. She kept thinking about how she would be feeling in a pickup truck carrying a load like that.

Then Delmer got a telephone call. In one day, the available airplanes and schedules had changed. The company was now using a different type of aircraft that could not carry a container the size of the antenna.

That afternoon, four different people, in two different states, were on the phones looking for an air carrier that would ship a 21-foot, 178-pound antenna from Portland, Oregon, to New York City. The fastest company found would guarantee its arrival by Wednesday, April 11—one day after the deadline. If the antenna was not in place and working by midnight, April 10, the entire project would be over. Everything already completed would have been done in vain. The fate of Channel 29 would be decided in the next few hours! There was special prayer at the Van Center in New York, and of course, many were praying in Oregon, asking God to intervene again.

By Thursday afternoon, the antenna manufacturing company had found a trucking company that owed them a favor and "happened" to be sending a truck to the New York City area. It would be traveling night and day and would take the antenna, if it were in Portland by 5:30 p.m. that afternoon to meet the trucker's departure schedule. *Thank you, God, for another miracle,* Evelyn prayed.

That evening Delmer called Pastor Bremmer to let him know the antenna was on a truck heading for New York City.

Monday morning came. The Van Center had just two days to have the TV station up and running and have the information in the office of the FCC. Pastor Bremmer, with five other men, arrived at the freight pickup location just outside the John F. Kennedy International Airport about 5:45 a.m. that morning. When they got to the pick-up location, one of the men spotted the box. Praise the Lord!! The antenna had arrived!! While the paper work was being completed, the men carried the antenna to the truck.

During the next several hours that 178-pound antenna was lifted and put into place. At 5:30 p.m. that evening, it was ready to be turned on. It had not been tested. Would it work? The switch was flicked, and it worked!!! After a few adjustments, someone said, "Check and see if you can see it on a TV. At 5:45 p.m., Pastor Bremmer turned on a portable TV in his van. He set the TV for Channel 29, and it worked!!! It was "a dream come true." Many, who had dreamed of this in the face of great odds and seeming impossibilities, saw their dreams come true.

When the lawyer, Don Martin, was called to send in the application to the FCC, Pastor Bremmer learned about a missing piece of technical information that was needed for the license. Starting around 6:00 a.m. on April 10—the last day—Pastor Bremmer began looking for the engineer who could provide the data needed. By that afternoon, the information was all taken care of, and Pastor Bremmer called Don Martin nine hours before the permit expired. Nine hours!! In less than half a day that TV station would have disappeared.

CHAPTER 29

Back in Oregon, Dave and Ann Reed were retiring and planned to move to sunny Arizona. Better Life Television needed a new manager, more equipment, and a new station.

The new station, Channel 30, was a commercial full-power station—ten times more powerful than any present channel owned by BLTV. The cost was high, but it would provide legal right to be on cable in all of southern Oregon.

The Better Life Television Board talked over the problems involved, thought about the money that would need to be raised, and decided this project was too big, too expensive, and could not be done. Therefore, the board voted to not pursue Channel 30 any further and to drop the whole project before any more money was "wasted" on it.

Delmer could not sleep that night. By morning he had made a decision. He would call another BLTV board meeting. "The possibilities are endless if we can get this station," he argued. "Surely God wants us to have this station. We serve a big God. He can make it happen. We must go forward."

Another vote was taken, and this time it was voted to go ahead and try to start Channel 30. Several board members were very upset—two board members resigned. Was working to get Channel 30 really what should be done? What if they couldn't raise the money?

Delmer had no question. "Yes, of course. This way we can be on cable. It is the only way to go."

Three other entities had applied for Channel 30. The FCC planned to put the permit for a license for Channel 30 up for auction among the four different applicants with the starting bid at two hundred thousand dollars. The other applicants did not want to use the channel—they had applied so they could sell it for a good price.

A corporation was formed consisting of all of the applicants for Channel 30. Now there was only one nucleus asking for Channel 30—the newly formed corporation. The FCC awarded this corporation the permit to make the station. The four applicants, who were now the nucleus of this corporation, worked among themselves on the procedures of selling the station to BLTV. It was agreed that the permit for a license for Channel 30 was worth five hundred thousand dollars.

There were numerous conference calls between Pastor Bob, Delmer, Don Martin, Better Life Television's lawyer in Washington DC, and the other three applicants with each of their lawyers, working out the details of selling Channel 30 to Better Life Television. Finally, the papers were ready to be signed. But first, BLTV had to secure the money to pay one hundred and twenty-five thousand dollars to each of the other three applicants who were a part of the corporation.

God touched the hearts of many unselfish people, and big sacrifices were made to raise the money. Each applicant was paid off, and the new corporation was dissolved. Better Life Television was now the owner of a permit for a full-power television license—or was it?

Day after day, week after week, and month after month, they waited for the license permit to come from the FCC. Pastor Bob and Delmer were told the permit would be coming "in a week," "next week," and "in a few weeks,"—but it never came. Finally, the man at the FCC got tired of talking with Delmer or Pastor Bob, and he stopped returning their telephone calls.

What could they do now? Precious time was being lost. God was their only hope, and they took these problems to Him in prayer. Delmer contacted his congressman, explained the situation, and asked him if he could do anything about it. After working with the congressman, Delmer was informed that he would receive a telephone call from the FCC the next week.

Monday came, and they anxiously awaited the phone call. Tuesday, Wednesday, and Thursday went slowly by without any word from the FCC. Friday afternoon, while Evelyn and Delmer were gone for a little while, the man from the FCC called. Returning home, Evelyn checked her answering machine. "Hello, this is Mr. (and he gave his name) returning Mr. Wagner's call." There was a moment's wait and then CLICK—the phone call was over as far as that man was concerned.

However, Delmer and Evelyn's answering machine was still on and was picking up what three men—probably back in Washington, DC—were saying. They were communicating via conference call or speaker phone.

"They cannot cover the territory that Mr. Wagner says they will be covering," one man said. "This license is for 80,000 watts, and he plans to run just 10,000 watts. There is no way he can cover the territory he says he will."

"Have you ever been out there in Oregon?" someone else asked. "They have high mountains."

"But there is no way Better Life Television can reach the territory that is supposed to be reached with this license using only that much power."

"You must notice that they have several stations and with the mountains like they are, the only way they can reach the people is by going from one station to another. That way they can cover the territory," insisted the second man.

They talked a little longer about Channel 30, and it was obvious that although the first man, the man Delmer and Pastor Bob had been working with, had not even planned to let them have the permit for a license for Channel 30, he was now convinced that maybe Better Life Television could reach the territory that it said it would be covering. As soon as the men started talking about some other television station, the answering machine turned off.

Now they knew why they had not received the license permit for Channel 30. **The FCC was not planning to give it to BLTV.** They would not need to if BLTV could not cover the territory assigned to it. Then the license could be sold to someone else. The FCC is very particular. Everything must follow the rules exactly. Evelyn trembled when she thought about the fact that BETTER LIFE TELEVISION could have lost all the money invested in Channel 30!!

Pastor Bob and Delmer listened to that telephone conversation over and over as they made their plans on how to approach the FCC. They hired an engineer to map out the actual coverage of the other stations that were going to be used, and it was sent to the FCC to show them how Better Life Television was covering the territory for Channel 30.

CHAPTER 30

Evelyn sat at her computer. The FCC had requested that some forms be filled out and sent to them, proving that Better Life Television owned the stations they had owned for years—minus the months they had been in Christian Life Broadcasting's name. The forms were long and very difficult to complete, for Evelyn at least. She did not do well under pressure, and these forms were due the next day.

She picked up the phone. "Delmer, you have to come home. I've never filled out forms on the Internet before. It isn't working."

Delmer was up on some mountain working on another "emergency" to get one of the stations back on the air again.

"Call 3ABN, and ask for Flo Cunningham," he replied. "She will help you. I don't know much more about this than you do."

Evelyn called Flo who found the forms with her computer and walked Evelyn through the hard parts. Now she could finish on her own, couldn't she? No. She had to call again and again. Flo was kind and patient when Evelyn called several times during the next few hours, and then—*Oh!*—*Oh dear!!*—*OH NO!!! What in the world did I do now? Everything was gone!!*

Well, I can't just sit here and cry. Something has to be done, she thought. She dried her tears and again called Flo who tried to walk her through the procedure of finding the nearly filled out forms. It was no use. They had disappeared! By now it was time for Flo to go home, but she promised Evelyn that she would stay late and fill out the forms for Better Life Television and see that they were sent to the FCC in time.

"Oh, thank you, God, for people like Flo." Evelyn laid her head on the desk, and tears of relief fell on the papers spread before her.

The powers of evil had been working hard to keep Better Life Television from obtaining Channel 30, but God had His "angels" working for Him, and Evelyn felt that Flo was one of them.

A few days later, on October 2, 2001, that precious permit from the FCC for Channel 30 was in their hands. Ten days later, after four years of planning, praying, negotiating, sacrificing, and working long hours, BLTV started broadcasting on Charter Cable, Channel 30!! It covered Medford, Grants Pass, and Rogue River. There was no doubt in anyone's mind that it was God who had arranged all things so BLTV—now called KBLN—could own a full-power station. KBLN is the first full-power TV station in Grants Pass and Josephine County and the first full-power affiliate of 3ABN in the world.

CHAPTER 31

Ron and Marta Davis were jolted awake at 4:30 a.m. when the violent 1994 earthquake of Northridge, California, hit. It was a terrifying experience with the electricity going off, furniture flying around, and shattering glass going everywhere. A major part of their home was destroyed and had to be rebuilt. They lost so much during those few terrible moments. However, the next Sunday morning at church, Marta was thinking, "They can take all of that away, but they cannot take away my relationship with God."

Both Ron and Marta had been raised in non-Christian homes. They lived for the weekends. On the weekends, they went water skiing and did a lot of socializing with friends. This usually included some drinking, and for Ron, ended with more drinking than he intended. Marta drank a glass of wine at dinner and another glass or two in the evening to be able to cope and relax a little. She thought the Bible was full of fables and fairytales. She said they were agnostics because they had never known anything else, and had never had the privilege of getting acquainted with the Lord.

When one of Ron's friends became a Christian, Ron felt irritated to think his friend had stopped social drinking with him and would not do some of the things they had done together in previous times. But as a born-again Christian, this friend shared literature with Ron who noticed there was a big change in his friend's life. From this literature, Ron learned about prophecy. It was exciting to learn that there was *Someone* who knew what was going to happen and was bold enough to say something.

About this time, Ron changed jobs and started riding to work with another born-again Christian. They had a long commute, and his friend shared his excitement and new-found faith. When these friends invited Ron and his family to an Easter Sunday sunrise service, they decided to go. The whole family accepted Jesus as their personal Savior when a call was made that Sunday morning—all except Marta. She had not had the same exposure to the Bible that Ron had.

Their children, who were now about ten and thirteen years old, had heard Bible Stories from a neighbor, so they were ready to surrender their lives to the Lord. This neighbor also told Marta, years later, that every day she went outside and saw the Davis' house, she had prayed for the whole family. God heard those prayers and lead the Davis family gently and slowly into the knowledge of His love.

Marta became curious about the Bible and started reading it. Soon she became acquainted with Jesus as she kept studying and learned that the Bible was truly the word of God. When another call was made for all of those who wanted to accept Jesus to raise their hand, Marta was ready. Jesus filled her heart with joy and a living relationship with Him. Then, she wondered how she had ever lived without Him. Now she could turn to the Lord with any problem, whatever it was. She could talk to the Master of the Universe, and He cared!! God also showed them in many ways that He is able to answer their personal prayers.

Ron and Marta continued reading the Bible from cover to cover. Their lives changed, and Ron said, "Now I was free." He was free from his old habits, and it was a great feeling.

Ron's friends would tell him, "Now you can't drink and

do the things you used to do."

But he didn't see it that way. He thought, *I am free! I am free from all of those things!!*

They could not see Jesus doing some of the things they had been doing, and if Jesus didn't do them, they didn't want to be doing them either. Proverbs 3:5 and 6 was a verse in the Bible that meant a lot to them. "Trust in the Lord with all thine heart; and lean not unto thine own understanding. In all thy ways acknowledge him, and he shall direct thy paths." Ron felt that if the Bible said it, they needed to apply it.

They spent the next sixteen years working in their church. However, there were many things they did not understand. Because of their close relationship with God, they knew He would teach them the truth as they studied His word. They were both convinced that God had a special work He wanted them to do.

When they moved to Grants Pass, Oregon, to be near their children and beloved granddaughter, they started watching Better Life Television. Ron wasn't much into watching Christian television because of all the glitz and glitter, but this program was different. "You must see this," he told Marta.

This program was completely off the wall with the preacher asking the question, "Is the Devil in charge of hell?" They wrote down the texts provided and looked them up. They were surprised to learn that the Bible confirmed what this preacher said. Soon they were watching KBLN more and more and studying the texts given. Those preachers were telling just exactly what the Bible said!!

Ron went to see his pastor at the Sunday church he attended. They were good friends and still are. They could talk about anything. Ron had a lot of confidence in this learned man. However, Ron felt that the Bible was the all-important truth—the last word so to speak—and if the Bible said it that was what he was going to go by.

Soon they were going to the Seventh-day Adventist church on Sabbath to learn what the Bible said and also going to their former church because they had so many lovely friends there. They were like sponges soaking up the new things they learned. The nagging question of what happens to a person when he or she dies was cleared up when they learned that a person doesn't live forever in hell or heaven after dying but that death is like a sleep until Jesus returns to awaken the dead.

Ron and Marta became "snowbirds," living in Grants Pass in the summer and going south in the winter. The last winter they spent in Mexico, they found a small Seventh-day Adventist church where they went to worship on Sabbath. There they learned the troubles and persecution a person can receive for being a member of this "different" denomination. This did not deter them, and they joined the Grants Pass Seventh-day Adventist Church that summer after returning from Mexico.

Now with KBLN on cable, many more people were watching the programs. More and more people were being baptized because of the station. Everything kept expanding. When the need arose for a station manager, some people asked Ron and Marta why they did not apply for the job.

Unknown to anyone, they began seeking the Lord to show them what to do. They decided that if anyone else mentioned that they should be the new managers of the television station, they would take it as a sign that the Lord wanted them to do it. Very soon after this decision, two people, at different times, came to them suggesting that they be the new managers at BLTV. They had put out a fleece to God to know what they should do, and He had answered. So, they let Better Life Television know that they would be willing to be the new managers.

They were planning to manage the station for a short time until someone else was found, and then they could go forward with whatever God wanted them to do. Now they are looking at it as this *is* what God wanted them to do. God had already handpicked Ron and Marta Davis to be the managers of Better Life Television.

CHAPTER 32

No one knew on September 2002 when *Puppet Parade,*a children's program, was inaugurated at KBLN that it would be aired on Trinity Broadcasting Network on "Smile of a Child network." The letters from little children everywhere were precious and heartwarming. The program, full of music and stories for small children, focuses on practical lessons in courtesy and the wonderful love of God. The Hope Channel also began broadcasting *Puppet Parade* around the world.

As KBLN continued to grow, it outgrew its available accommodations and more room was needed. In 2002, Maranatha workers arrived to help with the construction of new offices and a room for filming the local programs, remodeling, and other expansions of the building.

In 2005, Maranatha workers returned to make more space for the engineering department and a nice conference room, which was later turned into more offices as the growth of KBLN demanded.

Another helicopter was used to lift cement, the transmitter tower, and tools up Tin Pan Peak preparing for the new Channel 17. Many volunteers came to help, climb the mountain, and do whatever else was necessary for the big day.

New transmitters were installed—Coos Bay, Roseburg, Cave Junction, and Merlin. Delmer would drive around the countryside with a little TV by his side checking to see where a signal was coming in. After one of these experiences,

Evelyn insisted on doing the driving.

"You may be a better driver," she ran around to the driver's side, "but I am safer because I am watching the road."

Other transmitters were added for Klamath Falls, Yreka, and Shasta City. Before the transmitters were set up for the cable company to broadcast KBLN to Crescent City, Gold Beach, and the Brookings area, Evelyn went with Delmer to Camp Six Mountain. He climbed a tower and tried to figure out a way for the signal to go to Crescent City. The signal was picked up from Eight Dollar Mountain and sent to Camp Six Mountain above Gasquet, California. Now it needed to go to the coast. This link would go straight to the cable company. The cable company would then send KBLN programs into the homes of the people.

While sitting in the car trying to keep warm on the mountaintop, Evelyn pulled her coat tightly around her. Delmer was still up the tower and was trying to look straight to the coast as the wind whistled around him. As the wind grew stronger, Evelyn wondered if he would ever finish his task. Finally he climbed down the tower. "I think I have this figured out. We had better drive to Crescent City and check it out." Delmer was about to get into the car.

A man who had just driven up the mountain stopped his truck beside the car. "I suppose you know you have a flat tire." He pointed at their car.

"Oh, no, I didn't. Thanks for telling me." Delmer opened the trunk of the car. "Not again!" he mumbled to himself as he proceeded to change tires.

"It is too late to go to the coast this evening," he said as he climbed into the car. "I need to come back tomorrow, anyway."

"What did you mean by 'not again'?" Evelyn looked out

the window when they started down the road that was covered with sharp rocks just waiting to puncture some innocent person's tire.

"That is because I ruined a tire the last time I came up here." Delmer tried to miss the biggest rocks, and Evelyn watched the sun disappear behind the hills while darkness slowly made its way across the land.

KBLN Channel 30 is on Dish Network and also Direct TV, reaching homes in Lake, Klamath, Jackson, Josephine, and Curry counties in southern Oregon and Modoc and Siskiyou counties in northern California.

KBLN is also reaching the world through the internet with local programs: *Time Out, Better Life Today, Josephine Journals, Feature Presentations, Signs of the Times, Puppet Parade*, and the local church service.

Airing the local church service Sabbath afternoon and Sunday morning draws people from the community into the church. They seem to feel that they know the pastor after watching and listening to him week after week. It is fun meeting these people—new guests come to visit the church almost every Sabbath. KBLN is making a major difference in the community and to many people around the world.

The year 2006 showed startling results revealing that churches in KBLN's viewing area in southern Oregon experience 40 percent more new membership growth than the churches in the balance of the Oregon Conference. This same year *Puppet Parade* went to Central America to be translated into Spanish and to be used on the huge network of cable systems in South America.

After three years of negotiations, equipment purchases, and adjustments, KBLN went on Almega Cable Channel 52 in Shady Cove and surrounding areas.

In 2006, a full-power television station located in Roseburg, Oregon—with a low-power station in Eugene, KTVC and KAMK-LP package—went up for sale. The owners were not making enough money to keep the four million dollar stations operating. What an opportunity if only KBLN could afford those stations. It would double the viewing audience, and many more people would learn of the love of God. Ron negotiated with the owners, and they agreed to sell the two stations for 2.7 million. Would God bring in the money? *Would He?* Ron Davis serves a big God. He believed God wanted Better Life Television to have those stations. But time passed, and the stations were sold to another party. Still, Better Life Broadcasting Network, as it is now called, continued to grow, keeping many full-time workers and dozens of volunteers busy.

CHAPTER 33

"This construction permit to set up a television station in Tillamook, Oregon, will expire in only three weeks," Ron told Delmer. "The price was reasonable, but we will have to act quickly."

Delmer and Evelyn jumped into the car and headed for Tillamook late Sunday afternoon on June 3, 2007. "We will go as far as we can and then just get a motel," he said as they headed up I-5.

Soon it became dark, but Delmer was not ready to stop for the night. This was an emergency. There was little time to get this station on the air. Their car turned off the freeway and headed over the mountains to highway 101.

"I see a shortcut to Tillamook." Evelyn had pulled the tiny flashlight from her purse and was studying the map. "I think we can save quite a few miles if we take it."

The road had more curves than the map showed—a lot more curves! Delmer drove mile after mile on the narrow, crooked road.

"I think this must be a beautiful drive in the daylight." Evelyn tried to encourage her husband as she looked out the window watching the fog roll in.

By now it was past time to stop for the night, but where? There were no motels. The only thing to do was drive forward—hour after hour—and mile after slow tedious mile. Evelyn prayed for safety as Delmer drove. She knew her advice to take this road had not been the wisest recommendation she had ever given.

"Look for a motel." They had finally come to the end of the zigzagging road and were heading up highway 101. It was hard to see where they were as they entered Tillamook and saw a place to stay.

"There must be a fire here or policemen!" Delmer exclaimed as he brought the car to a stop.

Evelyn looked around. Flashing red lights pierced the foggy darkness.

"You must be very lost or very drunk," an officer said after walking up to the car. He asked to see Delmer's driver's license. "What are you doing here, anyway?" he questioned.

"I am looking for a motel, and we came here searching for a site to put up a television station," he told the police officer. After a bit of small talk, the officer said, "Well, you have found a motel, and good luck on your television station." Then he was gone.

Thank you, Lord. We surely don't need a ticket, Evelyn thought. What had they done wrong? Run a stop sign? Gone the wrong way on a one-way street? She was glad they never found out.

The next morning, they stopped at a radio station that rented a site on the tower. The manager gave them a key to a locked gate so they could drive to the top of the mountain. When they took the key back to the radio station, no one was able to contact the man who was in charge of renting sites on the tower. They drove to the address of the man's office. It had been closed for some time. However, they had an address to his home in Seaside.

They drove to Seaside. *Why won't he answer his telephone?* After wasting the rest of the day trying to find the place and using every method they knew to get in touch with this man, Evelyn was ready to go home; but Delmer did not want to give up. He didn't plan to let anything stop him from going forward on this project.

They drove to a little store to get something to eat and saw a man walk out of the building and get into a telephone company truck. Delmer rushed across the parking lot to the truck and showed the driver the address in his hand. The man looked at the paper and shook his head. He then studied some maps and smiled. "You will never be able to find that street. Just wait. I am about to get off work. You can follow me. I will take you right to the place."

They followed the truck up highway 101, down a narrow road, and around a bay, or lake, or whatever it was. Finally they came to the house situated on the short little street where the manager lived. His wife was very friendly, but the man had sort of disappeared. She didn't know where he was.

What were they to do now? They stopped to pray, and God answered in the form of some dedicated, unselfish members of the Seventh-day Adventist church in Tillamook who were willing to have the antenna placed on the roof of their home. *Thank you, God.*

It took several days to get the permit changed by the FCC to the new location, but miracles were happening, and the work was completed one day before the deadline. Now there was another station in Oregon pouring out the message of the love of God.

"O praise the Lord, all ye nations: praise him all ye people. For his merciful kindness is great toward us: and the truth of the LORD endureth for ever. Praise ye the LORD" (Psalm 117).

CHAPTER 34

By 2008, Better Life Broadcasting Network had out-grown its space and needed more room. Again Maranatha workers came and 14,000 more square feet were added to the now large, comfortable studio building with three new offices in the front, more storage space, and also a large conference room that doubles for a workroom and lunchroom. This spacious room can accommodate all the Better Life board members during the monthly meetings.

On March 26, 2009, Better Life Broadcasting Network turned on the transmitter for Channel 42 in Astoria, Oregon. It is another miracle of God to see this become a reality. This station will broadcast 3ABN from Long Beach, Washington, to Seaside, Oregon. All three churches in the area will benefit from this new coverage. The Astoria station is the sixteenth over-the-air broadcast station that Better Life Broadcasting Network owns and operates.

God has performed many miracles for Better Life Broadcasting Network—and He isn't through with it yet. Ron continued to feel that God wanted BLBN to have stations KTVC and KAMK-LP. Countless prayers ascended to God over this matter. Ron persistently followed what was happening to the two stations. Wow!! The company that purchased the two stations declared bankruptcy in 2009, and Better Life Broadcasting Network offered to buy them for nine hundred and seventy-five thousand dollars.

On April 16, 2009, the official court appointed auction

took place for these two stations. Ron Davis, on a conference call with the court proceeding in Dallas, Texas, heard first-hand the granting of those two stations: **"Go-ing-going-gone; to Better Life Broadcasting Network!**

Congratulations, you are the new owners of KTVC and KAMK-LP!"

Ellen G. White so clearly summarizes our experience thus far in working for the Lord: "The means in our possession may not seem to be sufficient for the work; but if we will move forward in faith, believing in the all-sufficient power of God, abundant resources will open before us. If the work be of God, He Himself will provide the means for its accomplishment. He will reward honest, simple reliance upon Him. The little that is wisely and economically used in the service of the Lord of heaven will increase in the very act of imparting" (*The Desire of Ages*, p. 371).

It is hard for some of us to even imagine what God will do as He moves forward eliminating some of the challenges facing Better Life Broadcasting Network.

On July 31, 2009, BLBN became the official owner of KTVC and KAMK-LP when they paid $900,000 cash for these two stations which will double the potential viewing audience of Better Life Broadcasting Network to one million people.

Ron and Marta Davis, along with the four full-time workers and about 100 volunteers, serve a big God.

Several years ago they started praying for a television station in Portland, Oregon. A couple of stations came on the market for $3,000,000 plus, but they seemed too expensive. Then another station became available that would add two million potential viewers.

On June 24, 2009, Better Life Broadcasting Network signed a purchase agreement for that station after the going price dropped to $700,000. God is not finished yet.

What a wonderful God we serve! He has a thousand ways to help that we know nothing of as we "Go Forward" in His love.

FORWARD

by Evelyn Wagner

As we travel on life's highway
When nothing seems quite right
Like going down a tunnel
With no end in sight—
Let's go forward.

There are times our friends forsake us.
At least that's the way we feel.
We may wish we could stop going,
For everything seems uphill—
Let's go forward.

Christ is right beside us.
He knows our every care.
He loves to carry our burdens
And our happiness share—
Let's go forward.

There are times the scenery
Will take our breath away;
We have reached a lovely moment;
It's a place we'd like to stay—
Let's go forward.

Eternal riches are ready
With pleasures too vast to be told.
All heaven is longing to greet us,
Waiting at the end of the road—
LET'S GO FORWARD.

INVISIBLE LEADERSHIP STORIES

By Evelyn Wagner

STORIES MY DADDY TOLD ME begins the series with Evelyn's great-great-grandfather, a Scottish soldier, being shipped to America from Scotland to join the British in the American Revolution. Instead, he and his companions joined George Washington and fought to help free the new country from the British rule. Evelyn's great-grandfather sailed around the world many times placing American Ambassadors in other countries. Follow God's leading in the life of her grandfather as he joined a wagon train to go west, became a friend of the great leader Chief Sitting Bull, and later learned to know the God Who had been leading all his life. Watch as God saved her father and family from thieves, financial failure, and potential robbers.

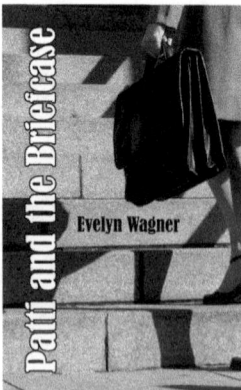

PATTI AND THE BRIEFCASE tells stories of a very shy bride going to Canada with her new husband to sell books. Stories too frightening and embarrassing for Evelyn to tell using her real name, she uses the name "Patti," the pet name her father called her when she was just a little girl.

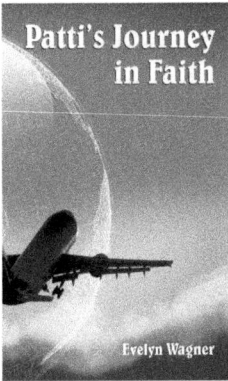

PATTI'S JOURNEY IN FAITH begins at Walla Walla College (University now) with a young couple named Delmer and Evelyn, but known as Del and Patti, in this setting. Travel with them in their struggle to serve their Lord in the challenges of going to college and then starting a new business. This story reveals a life of love, courage, disappointment, laughter, and discovery with the overarching theme of the gracious nearness of God.

FORWARD was the only way to go when Delmer and Evelyn stepped out in faith to start Christian television stations. God opened doors while the enemy built walls that seemed to shut down all progress. Watch God perform miracles when His people are willing to step FORWARD in faith.

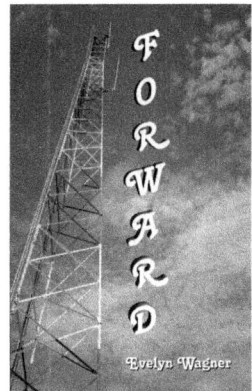

We invite you to view the complete
selection of titles we publish at:

www.TEACHServices.com

Scan with your mobile
device to go directly
to our website.

Please write or email us your praises, reactions, or
thoughts about this or any other book we publish at:

TEACH Services, Inc.
P U B L I S H I N G
www.TEACHServices.com

P.O. Box 954
Ringgold, GA 30736

info@TEACHServices.com

TEACH Services, Inc., titles may be purchased in bulk for
educational, business, fund-raising, or sales promotional use.
For information, please e-mail:

BulkSales@TEACHServices.com

Finally, if you are interested in seeing
your own book in print, please contact us at

publishing@TEACHServices.com

We would be happy to review your manuscript for free.

www.ingramcontent.com/pod-product-compliance
Lightning Source LLC
Chambersburg PA
CBHW060542100426
42742CB00013B/2425